WILLIAM BLAKE: SONGS OF INNOCENCE AND OF EXPERIENCE

WILLIAM BLAKE

Songs of Innocence and of Experience

Edited with an Introduction and Notes by
ANDREW LINCOLN

BLAKE'S ILLUMINATED BOOKS
Volume 2
General Editor DAVID BINDMAN

The William Blake Trust / Princeton University Press

WILLIAM BLAKE: *Songs of Innocence and of Experience*

ISBN 0-691-069360 (cloth)

Published by Princeton University Press
41 William Street, Princeton, New Jersey 08540
in conjunction with the William Blake Trust

Typesetting by Gloucester Typesetting Services
Printed in Great Britain by Balding & Mansell

© 1991 The Tate Gallery and the William Blake Trust

Library of Congress Cataloging-in-Publication Data

Blake, William, 1757-1827.
 Songs of innocence and of experience: shewing the two contrary
states of the human soul / William Blake: edited with an
introduction and notes by Andrew Lincoln.
  p.   cm. - - (Blake's illuminated books: v. 2)
 Includes bibliographical references.
 ISBN 0-691-06936-0: $59.50
 I. Lincoln, Andrew II. Title. III. Series: Blake, William.
1757-1827. Illuminated books; v. 2.
 PR4144.S6 1991   91-25620
 821'.7 — dc20   CIP

Contents

General Editor's Preface

THIS VOLUME is the second in the new series of facsimiles of Blake's Illuminated books to be produced by the Blake Trust, and it follows Professor Morton Paley's edition of *Jerusalem*. With *Jerusalem* there was no problem of choice of which copy to reproduce: the Mellon version, as the only completely coloured copy, was the unavoidable one. With *Songs of Innocence and of Experience* the situation is quite different. The book did have a following in Blake's own time, with the result that there are now extant some twenty-six copies of *Songs of Innocence* alone and more than twenty copies of the combined *Songs of Innocence and of Experience*. The choice is further complicated by the fact that before the completion of *Songs of Experience* and perhaps slightly later, *Songs of Innocence* was published separately. There is also a great range of variation in the order of the plates and in what plates are included or omitted, or put in either *Innocence* or *Experience*. The colouring may also vary substantially: in some copies of *Experience* it is applied by a colour-printing process; in others it is barely tinted on the surface, while in late copies it may have the richness of a medieval manuscript. There is, therefore, no ideal or exemplary copy of *Songs of Innocence and of Experience*, but by the last decade of Blake's life, to which the present copy belongs, the order of the plates and the general style of the colouring were more or less settled.

The choice of which copy of the book to reproduce for this edition was based on two criteria: we wanted to reproduce a particularly fine copy, and one that was relatively unfamiliar. On both these grounds the King's College copy has an indisputable claim. Because of its fascinating provenance and the fact that it has rarely been seen by the general public, it had acquired a particular aura of its own. Each plate has a watercolour border added by Blake himself, and though there is no reason to suppose, as has often been claimed, that it was 'Blake's own copy', it shows evidence of the highest degree of care on the artist's part.

This edition broadly follows the formula established in Professor Paley's edition of *Jerusalem*, and contains an introduction and commentary, and also a section of reproductions allowing the reader to obtain an idea of the variations to be found in other copies of *Innocence and Experience*. The Blake Trust is grateful to the editor of this volume, Dr Andrew Lincoln, and to all the other participants who have brought expertise and hard work to the task of achieving the best possible standard of reproduction that modern methods will allow. As with *Jerusalem* John Commander has been at the centre of this endeavour. We are also grateful to the Provost and Fellows of King's College, Cambridge for permission to reproduce their copy of *Songs of Innocence and of Experience* and for the assistance and support given by Mr Peter Jones, King's librarian, and his staff in helping to produce an edition worthy of the original.

DAVID BINDMAN

Foreword

I AM GRATEFUL to the Council of King's College, Cambridge for their agreement to publish their copy of *Songs of Innocence and of Experience* and especially to Mr Peter Jones, Librarian of King's College, for his unfailingly courteous assistance. The following individuals have provided information or answered queries: Detlef Dörrbecker, Robert N. Essick, Paul Ritchie, Joseph Viscomi and David Womersley. I should also like to thank David Bindman for his advice and encouragement, John Commander of The William Blake Trust for his help in seeing this work through the press, and my wife, Margarette Smith, for her support and patient criticism.

ANDREW LINCOLN
London
April 1991

Abbreviations

BB *Blake Books*, edited by G. E. Bentley, Jr. (Oxford, 1977)

BR *Blake Records*, edited by G. E. Bentley, Jr. (Oxford, 1969)

E   *The Complete Poetry and Prose of William Blake*, edited by David V. Erdman, commentary by Harold Bloom (New York, 1988)

IB *The Illuminated Blake*, edited by David V. Erdman (London, 1975)

K   *Blake, The Complete Writings*, edited by Geoffrey Keynes (London, 1972)

L   *The Letters of William Blake, with Related Documents*, edited by Geoffrey Keynes (Oxford, 1980)

Introduction

IN HIS OWN lifetime Blake's *Songs of Innocence and of Experience* was known only to those lucky enough to own, or have access to, one of the rare illuminated copies produced by the author himself.[1] Some twenty-four copies of the combined *Songs* have survived, and four copies of *Songs of Experience*, while twenty-six copies of the separate *Songs of Innocence* are known – one recently discovered (by Detlef Dörrbecker) in the Bavarian State Library at Munich.[2] The total is much higher than for any other work Blake published himself, but seems small given the reputation the songs now hold. No doubt Blake's limited means of advertising and the method of production tended to restrict sales. Although the songs were addressed to 'Every child', they were expensive: in 1793 *Innocence* and *Experience* were advertised at a total price of 10 shillings; by 1827, the year of Blake's death, the price had risen to ten guineas (*E* 693, *K* 208, *L* 169). The contents might also have deterred some potential customers: the songs challenge traditional assumptions, sometimes obliquely, sometimes with a daring directness. From the outset of his career as a self-publishing author, Blake was radically at odds with much of the public he sought to reach.

The Two Contrary States of the Human Soul

Blake's 'Contrary States' of Innocence and Experience illuminate many areas of thought and feeling. Among other things, they direct attention to dualities at the heart of the Christian tradition. In the Bible there are many contrasting ideas and images which interpreters usually seek to harmonise. Divine power is associated with terror and with joy. God is presented as a transcendent being who demands obedience to moral law, and as a loving merciful being who becomes human. If the opening chapters look back to a lost intimacy with the Lord in a garden, others celebrate an ever present relationship with Him as a good shepherd. There are visions of a universal resurrection at the eventual termination of history, and of individual regeneration as a present reality. Redemption is associated with the death of the Saviour, and with His birth. In the *Songs* Blake presents comparable contrasts, not as elements of a coherent and unified system of belief, but as aspects of two contrary modes of vision that illuminate each other dialectically.

There is no definitive text of the *Songs*, and as some poems were transferred from Innocence to Experience general comments about either 'State' have to be related to particular arrangements of the poems. In the copy reproduced in this edition, all of the songs that feature a 'bardic' voice appear in Experience. The poems of Innocence focus

---

[1] Seven songs were published separately in Blake's lifetime. Benjamin Heath Malkin printed four in *A Father's Memoirs of his Child* (1806) ('Laughing Song', 'Holy Thursday', 'The Divine Image' and 'The Tyger'). Crabb Robinson also printed the Innocence 'Holy Thursday' and 'The Tyger', as well as 'The Garden of Love' and part of the 'Introduction' to Innocence, in the German *Vaterländisches Museum* 1 (January 1811). The Innocence 'Holy Thursday' was printed again in *City Scenes* [compiled by Jane and Ann Taylor] (1818). The Innocence 'Chimney Sweeper' appeared in James Montgomery's *Chimney-Sweepers' Friend and Climbing-Boys' Album* (1824) (*BR* 253–54, 421–47).

[2] The numbers given here do not include posthumous copies. The copies of *Songs of Experience* are listed among the combined copies of the *Songs* (as G, H, K and N) in *William Blake's Illuminated Books: A Census*, compiled by Geoffrey Keynes and Edwin Wolf 2nd (New York, 1953), and in *BB*. Two of them (K and N) appear to have been bound at one stage with Innocence plates. See *BB* 415–18.

on joyful and protective relationships, on the sense of common identity between individuals. In the awareness of shared happiness – present, remembered or anticipated – innocents triumph over loss, deprivation and the steady passage of time. Divinity here is an innate presence that becomes visible in the human form, a personal saviour 'ever nigh' who comforts the distressed. The landscape of Innocence is typically common ground: pastoral fields, valleys wild, the village green. But although this state of being is apparently idyllic, it is not without its limitations. Its ever ready comfort and security involve passivity, dependence, even at times a feeling of resignation. The possibility that Innocence might lead to entrapment is never confronted directly in the poems, but can often be sensed. In 'On Anothers Sorrow' (the last Innocence poem in this arrangement), the conviction that the divine comforter sits 'both night & day / Wiping all our tears away' anticipates the spiritual stalemate of some Experience poems, in which fears are increased and made habitual by weeping 'both night & day'.

In contrast to the steady faith of Innocence, Experience is a state of disillusionment in which distress breeds anger and a new kind of hope. In this state the prophetic consciousness appears, with its vision of a past 'Age of Gold' from which humanity has fallen, its tormented awareness of present error and cruelty, its hope of a universal resurrection 'In futurity'. While the Innocence poems dwell on pleasure and consolation, the poems of Experience emphasize the fearful selfishness of the human heart, and the confusion and tyranny that grow from attempts to rationalize this selfishness. A typical setting of Experience is the garden, the enclosed space in which the individual, withdrawn from the larger community, cultivates private desires. The garden of Experience inevitably recalls the myth of Eden, which in this perspective can be seen as the expression of a severely limited and limiting attitude to life. If the divinity of Innocence becomes 'an infant small' in order to bring comfort and joy to the world, the divinity of Experience is usually a figure of dread, a distant father who presides over repressive institutions and ideologies. The satirical drive of Experience thus strikes at the roots of 'ancient' tradition. But in doing so it exposes its own limitations. In Experience hope and repression seem intimately related: both spring from the conviction that humanity is fallen. The Holy Word who urges earth to arise has begun to sit in judgment on 'the lapsed Soul'. The prophetic consciousness seems bound by the conditions it strives with. The seer who anticipates the transformation of the 'desart wild' accepts 'a garden mild' as his ideal.

The *Songs of Innocence and of Experience* rarely offer simple choices – as between moral absolutes – but tend to emphasize the relativity of particular images and points of view. 'Mercy Pity Love and Peace' can reveal the innate divinity in human life, or mask the selfishness of the natural heart. To accept one view and refuse the alternative would be to turn away from an unpleasant truth or to accept a reductive view of human feeling. Some poems contain contradictory views within them, and as we shall see, Blake's technique generates ambiguities that repeatedly complicate interpretation. Few books offer such challenges with such a disarming appearance of simplicity.

Blake before the Songs

Blake was born on 28 November 1757. His father, a hosier in London's Soho, belonged to a class of tradesmen and artisans that preserved a long tradition of radical dissent.[3] We don't know what kind of religious instruction Blake received as a child, but it left him with a passionate interest in the Bible: in later life he cited Ezra and Isaiah as among the most important influences of his childhood (see *L* 20). In his youth he discovered the occult writings of Paracelsus and Boehme, which may have encouraged a radical questioning of Christian tradition. Boehme insisted that scripture should be read symbolically, and that institutional religion or 'Babel', with its 'Pageantries and Solemnities and Belly Ordinances' has 'stopped the Mouth of the Spirit of God'.[4] He argued that a dynamic opposition of positive and negative qualities is essential to life – a view that contrasts with the traditional understanding of good and evil as absolutes. Both Boehme and Paracelsus described the imagination as a divine, creative power.[5] Some of the ideas that became centrally important in Blake's work, including his view of 'contraries', and his belief in the prophetic significance of art, may have begun to take shape under the influence of these writers while he was still in his teens. His interest in the visionary writings of Emmanuel Swedenborg in the late 1780s was probably a renewal and extension of preoccupations already well established. Some other artists of the time are known to have shared comparable visionary interests.[6]

Blake's artistic promise had been recognized early by his father. At the age of ten he was sent to Henry Pars's drawing school, where he learned to develop his skills by copying prints in drawing books and casts of antique statuary. As he had no income, he had little chance of going on directly to become a professional painter. Instead, in August 1772 he was apprenticed to the antiquarian engraver James Basire, a move that would guarantee him a living. In October 1779, soon after his apprenticeship was completed, he was formally admitted to the Royal Academy.[7] Some of the works he exhibited at the Academy during the new few years are now lost, but they are known from other versions and their titles give a clear indication of his interest in prophetic subjects (they include 'War unchain'd by an angel, Fire, Pestilence and Famine following', and 'The Bard, from Gray'). His ambition is evident in the series of three large watercolours, 'The Story of Joseph' (now in the Fitzwilliam Museum, Cambridge).

While entry to the Academy must have fuelled Blake's hopes of establishing himself as an artist engraver, in the early eighties he began to win some recognition as a poet among his friends. John Thomas Smith 'often heard him read and sing several of his poems' at the 'converzationes' of Mrs Harriet Mathew. 'He was listened to by the

[3] For a detailed discussion of this background see E. P. Thompson, *The Making of the English Working Class* (Harmondsworth, 1968), pp. 28–58.

[4] *The Works of Jacob Behmen* (London, 1764), I, 182; III, 354.

[5] According to Paracelsus, all mental and physical activities are governed by the imagination: 'Imagination is the mover of my course', *Paracelsus his Achidoxes* (London, 1661), p. 8. For a fuller discussion of the influence of Boehme and Paracelsus on Blake, see Désirée Hirst, *Hidden Riches* (London, 1964), pp. 59–68, 95–9.

[6] The miniaturist Richard Cosway and the landscape painter P. J. de Loutherbourg shared an interest in Swedenborgianism. The engraver William Sharp became a follower of the contemporary prophets Richard Rogers and Joanna Southcott. See David Bindman, *William Blake: His Art and Times* (New Haven and Ontario, 1983), pp. 10–13.

[7] David Bindman notes 'He was enrolled as an engraver, but as engraving was apparently not taught at the school, this may have been an indication that he was not expected to serve his full term as a student'. *Blake as an Artist* (Oxford, 1977), p. 19.

company with profound silence, and allowed by most of the visitors to possess original and extraordinary merit' (*BR*, 26). Blake's friend John Flaxman, perhaps helped by Mrs Mathew, arranged for the printing of *Poetical Sketches* (1783), a collection of Blake's poems 'commenced in his twelfth, and occasionally resumed by the author till his twentieth year' (*BR* 25). The volume shows Blake's enthusiastic response to a wide range of poets from earlier centuries, including Chaucer, Spenser, Shakespeare and Milton, and it anticipates some of the distinctive features of his later work. Personification and pastoral are used to evoke a transforming, ecstatic vision of the divine in the natural ('To Spring', 'Song: Fresh from the dewy hill'). States of mental captivity are described from within ('How sweet I Roam'd', 'Mad Song'). Conflicting views play against each other without a resolution ('Contemplation'). The prose poem 'Samson', which leaves the hero poised ambiguously on the brink of disaster, is an early experiment in prophetic narrative. Blake's Samson can be seen as a type of the artist, who struggles against the materialism of his own age – and is doomed to be seduced by it before finally achieving his mission.[8] The vulnerability of the would-be deliverer suggests that spiritual capitivity is a state through which the strongest of mortals must pass.

By the late 1780s Blake may have come to feel that he was in danger of being spiritually enslaved by the taskwork of engraving, which left him financially dependent on the tastes of the commercial market. His artistic ambitions had proved difficult to harmonise with the need to make a living. As early as 1780 he had begun to earn money by engraving works of other artists. Two years later he married, increasing the need for regular income. In 1784 an attempt was made to raise a subscription for him to complete his artistic studies in Rome, but the scheme came to nothing. In the same year he attempted to set up a small print-selling and publishing business with his friend James Parker (once a fellow apprentice under Basire). The business venture may have promised financial independence but it was short-lived, and by 1787 Blake was engraving for other publishers again. As an artist he had failed to establish a wide reputation, and even as a professional engraver he had achieved only moderate success.[9] If the publication of *Poetical Sketches* raised hopes of gaining public recognition as a poet, the volume seems to have made little impression beyond his immediate circle.[10]

Illuminated Printing

Blake probably developed his own method of illuminated printing in the hope of finding an audience for his gifts as an artist and poet that might otherwise be denied to him. In a prospectus of October 1793 he claimed that the poverty and obscurity which have proverbially attended the labour of artists were 'never the fault of the public', but were due

[8] See 'Blake's Early Poetry', by Michael Phillips, in *Essays in Honour of Sir Geoffrey Keynes*, edited by Morton D. Paley and Michael Phillips (Oxford, 1973), pp. 16–26. As Phillips points out, the identification between Samson and the artist would have been suggested by the traditional identification of Milton with the hero of *Samson Agonistes*. For a fuller discussion of *Poetical Sketches* see Margaret Lowery, *Windows of the Morning* (New Haven, 1940) and Robert F. Gleckner, *Blake's Prelude* (Baltimore and London, 1982).

[9] In the 1780s he seems to have had a steady flow of work, but his failure to win commissions for Alderman Boydell's *Shakespeare Gallery* (apart from one plate which seems not to have been published) gives some indication of his position.

[10] For details of the *Poetical Sketches* project see Michael Phillips, 'William Blake and the "Unincreasable Club": The Printing of *Poetical Sketches*', *Bulletin of the New York Public Library* 79 (1976), pp. 6–18.

to the 'neglect of means to propagate' works of art: 'Even Milton and Shakespeare could not publish their own works' (*E* 692–3, *K* 207–8). He seems to have envisaged a direct relationship between artist and public, without the intervention of theatres, galleries or commercial publishers. The implied distrust of those who control the market parallels his distrust of religious institutions ('a system was formed, which some took advantage of' (*The Marriage of Heaven and Hell, E* 38, *K* 153).

The first indication of his interest in new methods of printing appears in the satirical fantasia *An Island in the Moon*, composed about 1782–85, which probably draws on his experience at Mrs Mathew's gatherings. Here Blake describes with some irony a scheme to reproduce an illuminated manuscript:

> Then said he I would have all the writing Engraved instead of Printed & at every other leaf a high finishd print all in three Volumes folio, and sell them a hundred pounds a piece. they would Print off two thousand (*E* 465, *K* 62)

The target here may be his friend George Cumberland, who had devised a method of reproducing handwriting from a copper plate.[11] But no doubt the passage also reflects Blake's own ambitions. Elsewhere in the manuscript there is evidence that he was already experimenting: on the back of page 16 the letters 'Bla' of his surname are transcribed in reverse, apparently an attempt at the mirror writing that would be needed to print direct from copper.[12] The method of 'illuminated printing' or relief etching he eventually devised not only allowed him to act as his own publisher – it allowed him to integrate text and illustration on a single plate, and it liberated him from some of the constraints imposed by the process of engraving. The design was probably drawn and painted directly onto the copper plate in an acid-resistant medium. That part of the surface left bare was eaten away when the plate was immersed in acid, leaving the design in relief. The raised image was then inked and printed on an etching press. As Joseph Viscomi notes, 'In relief etching, unlike engraving, Blake could freely conceive, compose and execute in terms of the same medium'.[13]

The first fruits of his invention are the small tracts known as *All Religions are One* and *There is No Natural Religion*, which were apparently etched around 1788.[14] These are clearly experimental works, in which Blake still seems to be learning the art of mirror writing.[15] They include a number of motifs that become familiar in the *Songs* – trees supporting vines, soaring birds, children with guardians, a piper. The relatively small plates show little of the freedom of line, or the fluid relationship between text and design, that Blake achieves in later works. But the tracts show how Blake intended to use his invention: they develop a distinction between the 'Poetic or Prophetic character' – the source of all knowledge, form and religion – and the 'Philosophical & Experimental'

---

[11] There were other comparable experiments in the 1780s: Franz Ignaz Joseph Hoffman, and Alexander Tilloch are known to have devised their own stereotype methods. See *BR* 32.

[12] See *An Island in the Moon*, edited by Michael Phillips (Cambridge, 1987), p. 12.

[13] *The Art of William Blake's Illuminated Books* (Manchester, 1983), p. 9.

[14] The statement in *The Ghost of Abel*, 'Blakes Original Stereotype was 1788' (*E* 272, *K* 32), is usually seen as a reference to one or more of these tracts. None of the surviving copies seems to have been printed this early.

[15] Some letters slope backwards, and some are even reversed.

character, which in itself can lead only to 'the same dull round' of existing knowledge (*E* 3, *K* 97). Illuminated printing is already a prophetic medium in which Blake sets out to challenge some of the fundamental assumptions of his own age.

Songs of Innocence

Songs of Innocence was first issued as a separate work, in 1789 according to the title-page. The process of composition must have extended over several years, as the collection includes three poems that first appeared in 'An Island in the Moon', and one that was transcribed in a copy of *Poetical Sketches*.[16] The 'Introduction' announces the work as a book for children:

> So I wrote
> Every child may joy to hear

Blake had already become involved in the rapidly expanding market for children's books. Early in his professional career he was commissioned to engrave designs for *The Speaker* (*c.* 1780), an anthology designed to 'facilitate the improvement of Youth in reading and Writing', and for Mrs Barbauld's *Hymns in Prose for Children* (1781). He probably had little sympathy with the educational aims of these books, or indeed with much of the children's literature written for the polite market.[17] But he seems to have known the market well. As many critics have noted, in the variety of its contents *Songs of Innocence* invites comparison with a range of other children's books available at the time, including collections of hymns for children, such as those by Isaac Watts, Charles Wesley or Anna Barbauld; educational playbooks such as William Ronksley's *The Child's Week's Work*, 1712; and emblem books such as John Wynne's *Choice Emblems . . . for the Improvement and Pastime of Youth*, 1772.

In the later eighteenth century, children's books were often illustrated, usually with an engraving or simple woodcut. Some pictures were even coloured with watercolours.[18] Many of the visual images in Blake's work have their counterparts in contemporary books: the shepherd with his pipe, the seated woman who shows a book to two children, the vine growing around the tree, the child lost in a wood, the mother watching her baby in its cradle, and – of course – children at play.[19] But Blake's integration of text and design goes far beyond the capacities of conventional printing methods. The relief etching process seems to have encouraged him to avoid blank spaces, to fill his margins with decorative motifs, to add the tiny leaves and figures that appear in or around the text of

---

[16] Early versions of the Innocence poems 'Holy Thursday', 'Nurse's Song' and 'The Little Boy lost' appear in *An Island in the Moon* (*E* 462–3; *K* 59–60). In one copy of *Poetical Sketches*, three pastoral poems were transcribed (not in Blake's hand), one of which is a version, probably earlier, of 'Laughing Song' (*E* 792, *K* 63).

[17] As J. H. Plumb says: 'the new children's literature was designed to attract adults, to project an image of those virtues which parents wished to inculcate in their offspring, as well as to beguile the child', 'The New World of Children in Eighteenth-Century England', *Past and Present* 67 (May 1975). For a survey of the educational assumptions that underlie eighteenth-century children's literature, see Zachary Leader, *Reading Blake's Songs* (London, 1981), pp. 1–36.

[18] Michael Phillips notes of John Wynne's *Choice Emblems*: 'in many surviving copies . . . a number of the plates have been coloured (though somewhat crudely) with water-colours . . .', 'William Blake's *Songs of Innocence and of Experience* from Manuscript Draft to Illuminated Book', *The Book Collector* 28 (1979), p. 37.

[19] See Robert Essick, *William Blake, Printmaker* (Princeton, 1980), pp. 138–9.

his songs.[20] This embellishment invites close exploration of each plate, and helps to make the hand coloured copies of the work look more like illuminated manuscripts than printed books.[21]

In the poems there is a comparable transformation of familiar conventions. The references to the shepherd, the Lamb, and to the 'maker' who comforts the distressed may recall the hymns of Charles Wesley and others, but there is no mention of sin or divine punishment. Several poems develop variations on the Christian theme 'Whoso dwelleth in love dwelleth in God' (*E* 599, *K* 87). But the theme is approached without conventional qualifications, in a way that tends to dissolve the traditional distinction between the human and the divine. Children's unselfconscious innocence is sometimes used to expose the limitations of adult perspectives. Indeed, the child-like vision of the poems may even challenge contemporary assumptions about poetic argument. The reader is drawn into a world in which ambiguous syntax and elusive ironies at once invite and frustrate a search for definite conclusions.

Songs of Experience

As the sequel to the Innocence series, *Songs of Experience* differs considerably in mood and perspective. We can see the work taking shape in the notebook Blake inherited from his brother Robert, who died in 1787. Most of the poems of *Experience* appear here, some in the early stages of composition. They are not accompanied by their designs, although at least three of the Experience designs (for the title-page, 'My Pretty Rose Tree' and 'London') were derived from a series of emblems sketched in the notebook under the title 'Ideas of Good and Evil'.[22] The last poem in the notebook sequence is a long lyric 'Let the Brothels of Paris be opened' which, as David Erdman has shown, alludes to events surrounding the career of La Fayette between 1789 and the late summer of 1792.[23] There are clear thematic relationships between some of the *Experience* poems and the other illuminated books offered for sale in the 1793 prospectus.[24] The bitterly ironical references to 'God & his Priest & King' show a new outspokenness in Blake's work, a new drive to expose the social consequences of error, which was no doubt prompted by the course of events in revolutionary France, and by the political turmoil in England. In reading through the notebook sequence and studying the revisions one can trace, as Michael Phillips says, 'the vision of *Experience* becoming sharper, more penetrating and more uncompromising with each stage'.[25] But Blake's concern with social and religious tyranny here is an extension of his interest in the habits of thought that

[20] Viscomi notes a 'tightly composed design needs to be etched less deeply than one with open areas', *The Art of William Blake's Illuminated Books*, p. 9.

[21] Bindman suggests that Blake may have had an acquaintance with the inheritors of the medieval tradition of illumination, such as the prayer books and devotional works of John Sturt. *Blake as an Artist*, p. 61.

[22] See *The Notebook of William Blake*, edited by David V. Erdman (Oxford, 1973).

[23] David V. Erdman, *Prophet Against Empire* (Princeton, 1977), pp. 182–8.

[24] Several other illuminated books were offered for sale in the prospectus: *The Marriage of Heaven and Hell, Visions of the Daughters of Albion, America* and *The Book of Thel*, as well as the small book of emblems, *The Gates of Paradise*. The last of these is in the style of an emblem book for children, while the pastoral *Thel* might also be thought of as a children's book.

[25] 'William Blake's *Songs of Innocence and of Experience* from Manuscript Draft to Illuminated Book', p. 58.

imprison individuals in 'the same dull round'. The notebook includes a 'Motto to the Song of Innocence & of Experience':

> The Good are attracted By Mens perceptions
>   And Think not for themselves
>   Till Experience teaches them to catch
> And to cage the Fairies & Elves
>
> And then the Knave begins to snarl
> And the Hypocrite to howl
> And all his good Friends shew their private ends
> And the Eagle is known from the Owl

Cruelty and repression are seen to be rooted in mental passivity; the conventional association of goodness with conformity and restraint is seen as both a symptom and a source of error. The Motto wasn't used, but its presence among the notebook poems gives a clear indication of how Blake saw the combined work. The use of 'Contrary States' was intended to make readers think 'for themselves'.

The Experience poems were printed in a format which parallels that of Innocence, with contrasting lettering (generally pseudoitalic as opposed to the upright roman miniscule usually found in Innocence).[26] Some were apparently etched on the back of Innocence plates.[27] The designs, like those of the earlier series, include motifs that appear in contemporary children's books – the game of shuttlecock and battledore (plate 40), the sooty sweep walking through a street (plate 37).[28] The illustration for 'Nurses Song' is comparable to one Blake designed and engraved for Mary Wollstonecraft's *Original Stories From Real Life* (1791).[29] The disarming resemblance to children's books quite belies the scope and complexity of the Experience poems.

The Combined Songs

In the combined work the parallel between the two series helps to focus attention on the differences: Innocence poems may be linked to their counterparts in Experience by identical or contrasting titles, while visual contrasts reinforce those in the text. The designs of Innocence make more use of flowing, curving lines, protective spaces, exuberant vegetation; in Experience spaces are often defined and fractured by bare branches. The etched images on the Innocence plates are usually delicate and finely detailed: the textures of fleeces, bark, furnishings and leaves are clearly represented, large surfaces are lightened by fine lines or stippling, while distance may be suggested by variations in shading or width of line. In the first plate of 'The Ecchoing Green' (figure 1), for example, the trunk and canopy of the central oak are carefully textured; the grass is

---

[26] The earliest copies of *Songs of Innocence* (copies A–G, I–J, X, *c.* 1789–93) include plates 2–27, 34–6, as well as 53 ('The School Boy') and 54 ('The Voice of the Ancient Bard'). The text on these plates is inscribed in upright miniscule roman letters, except on plate 54 where the text is in pseudoitalic. The Experience poems are usually inscribed in pseudoitalic. The exceptions are on plates 42 ('The Tyger'), 43 (only 'Ah! Sun Flower'), 46 ('London'), 49 ('A Poison Tree'), and 50 ('A Little Girl Lost': the first stanza).

[27] The evidence is discussed by Bentley, who concludes that 'at least six, and perhaps as many as twenty-two' Experience plates were etched in this way (*BB* 382).

[28] See Essick, *William Blake, Printmaker*, p. 138.

[29] David Bindman, *The Complete Graphic Works of William Blake* (London, 1978), no. 109.

shaded with horizontal lines that become bolder in the foreground; distant trees and bushes are finely etched behind the standing players. (Figures 1 to 12 appear after the plates of the *Songs*.) In places Blake includes 'white-line' work – very fine lines that appear white against the inked areas – as in the carpet on plate 17 (to suggest both the texture and the pattern of the weaving, see figure 2), or in the flame-like form on plate 18.[30] Such finishing is well suited to the light, transparent watercolour washes Blake used to colour the printed impressions in early copies. In later copies, like the one reproduced in this edition, the details of the printed impression are often obscured and replaced by dense overpainting. The etched images on the Experience plates generally have fewer details and show less concern with texture. The leafless trees are represented in bold outlines, their trunks shaded with a few unbroken patches. Where surface textures are represented, they usually differ from those in the Innocence plates. The scene with mother and child on plate 48 in Experience ('Infant Sorrow', figure 3) is comparable to the scene on plate 17 in Innocence ('A Cradle Song'), but the wicker of the crib is less tightly woven, while the carpet lacks the fine weave and the pattern of its Innocence counterpart. (On plate 48 of this copy, as on plate 17, Blake has painted a pattern on the carpet.) At the top of the Experience plate 45 ('The Little Vagabond') the tree bark was etched with a coarse, vertical grain quite unlike the horizontal patterning usually found in Innocence. Plates 34–6 and 53, which originally appeared in Innocence, are clearly distinguished from the other Experience plates by the style of their etching. The style of Experience is generally heavier and flatter.

VARIATIONS: ADDITIONS, TRANSFERS, ORDERING

Blake's conception of the *Songs* seems to have evolved through several stages. In the prospectus of October 1793, *Songs of Innocence* and *Songs of Experience* were advertised as separate works. Perhaps Blake assumed they would be easier to sell individually, although in practice it seems that the Experience poems were usually sold in combination with their Innocence counterparts.[31] When Blake combined the two series into a single collection in 1794, he transferred 'The Little Girl Lost' and 'The Little Girl Found' (plates 34–6) from Innocence to Experience.[32] In copies B–E these plates seem to have been printed with the other poems of Innocence, and as they were printed back-to-back, two other poems that normally appear in Innocence were transferred to Experience with them: 'A Dream' (copies B–D) and 'Laughing Song' (copy E). In copy E 'Laughing Song' appears twice, as it is also in Innocence. These transfers give a clear indication that the boundaries between the two 'States of the Human Soul' were not hard and fast in Blake's view. One early copy (A) lacks the general title-page and three of the Experience poems found in later copies ('A Little Boy Lost', 'A Little Girl Lost',

---

[30] These lines are produced by cutting through the protective medium on the copper plate with an etching needle or comparable tool, as in itaglio etching. Like the other unprotected areas, the lines are bitten when the plate is immersed in acid.

[31] Bentley notes: 'In seventeen copies of the *Songs* (A–I, K, N–T), *Experience* was produced separately from *Innocence*, as is demonstrated by the distinctly different sets of printing colours . . . numbers . . . and stab holes' (*BB* 381).

[32] In the 1793 prospectus, *Innocence* and *Experience* were said to contain twenty-five illuminated plates each. In none of the surviving combined copies does either *Innocence* or *Experience* have this number of plates. It seems likely that in 1793 Blake still included the three plates of 'The Little Girl' poems in *Innocence*. These plates are absent from the separate, colour printed copies of *Experience*.

and 'To Tirzah'). Three early copies (B–D) have an endplate showing a naked youth borne through the air by cherubs (plate a, see figure 4), perhaps introduced as a counterpart to the two frontispieces. These copies lack 'To Tirzah', which seems associated with other prophetic writings later than 1803.[33] Copy BB contains an additional poem, 'A Divine Image' (plate b), which is otherwise found only in copies printed after Blake's death (see figure 5).[34] Two songs, 'The School Boy' and 'The Voice of the Ancient Bard', were originally in Innocence, and appear there in early copies of the *Songs*; in later copies they appear in Experience. Their transfer means that in latest copies all of the poems of protest, and all which feature a 'bardic' voice, usually appear in Experience.

Apart from such additions and transfers there is considerable variation in the arrangement of the poems. Blake seems to have tried a different order for the plates with each new copy until about 1815, when he began to favour one arrangement, shared by six copies including the one reproduced here (copy W).[35] An undated document in Blake's hand shows 'The Order in which the *Songs of Innocence & of Experience* ought to be paged & placd,' but this order appears in only one copy (V), printed on paper with a watermark 1818 (see *L* 143–4).

VARIATIONS: PRINTING AND COLOURING

Variations in the colouring of the plates ensure that no two copies are quite alike. Within each copy of the *Songs* the print colour is usually consistent, although some contain more than one print colour.[36] Most are printed in brown or orange, but Blake sometimes used green, black or grey, and occasionally blue. The printed impression was in most cases subsequently coloured by hand.[37] Some Experience plates in a few copies were coloured partly or completely with opaque pigments that have a distinctive, reticulated surface (copies B, C, F, G, H, and T).[38] It has been shown that a comparable surface can be produced by painting over a printed impression when it is still wet, but most of these plates are thought to have been colour printed.[39] Blake may have painted the copper

[33] 'To Tirzah' seems related to the symbolism of *Milton*, *Jerusalem* and the revisions of *The Four Zoas*. This would suggest a date sometime after 1800, and possibly after 1803, for those copies in which this poem appears. But it is included in copy L, which has '1799/JS' inscribed on the recto of plate 2 – perhaps, says Bentley, an acquisition or early library mark. And it appears in Copy O, which may have been bound in 1797 (*BB* 417, 418).

[34] See Robert Essick, 'New Information on Blake's Illuminated Books', *Blake: An Illustrated Quarterly*, 15 (1981), 4–5.

[35] The other copies with this arrangement are U, X, Y, Z and AA. Bentley notes 'The plates of *Innocence* and the combined *Songs* were arranged in thirty-four distinct ways' (*BB* 386).

[36] Interpolation or collation accounts for the occurrence of more than one print colour in a copy. In copy S, for example, the Innocence plates are printed in black, the General Title-page and Experience plates in brown.

[37] Two copies of *Songs of Innocence* (*I, U*) and three copies of the combined *Songs* (M, O, Q) were left uncoloured. Bentley notes that Q has some grey and pale brown wash in Experience (*BB* 385 n. 1).

[38] The plates of Copy T apparently derive from two different copies. The colour printed Experience plates (28, 32–3, 38, 40–3, 47, 49–51), now known as T¹, were added to what must have once been a complete copy of the combined work, T². Fifty-two plates are now in the British Museum Print Room, eleven in the National Gallery of Canada.

[39] In Copy B some Experience plates have an opaque black shading which may have been painted rather than printed. The evidence is discussed by Joseph Viscomi in 'Recreating Blake's Illuminated Prints: The Facsimiles of the Manchester Etching Workshop', *Blake: An Illustrated Quarterly*, 19 (1985), 4–23 (p. 8).

plate, colouring both the relief image and the lowered areas, and then transferred the paint to the paper. The 'printed' colours were sometimes retouched to sharpen drapery folds and other details, but clarity and subtlety of line seem less important than the textured impression created by areas of dense colour (see figure 6). Plates finished in this way may offer a striking contrast with the plates of Innocence, which are invariably finished in watercolour. The effects are sometimes extraordinary, as in the image of the 'Tyger' in copy T (figure 7). The 'colour printed' plates may have been among the earliest copies of Experience produced. No Innocence plates are coloured in this way, and as Gerald Bentley notes, 'since pl. 34–6, 52–4 were not colour printed, it seems likely that the colour printing took place before pl. 34–6 were added to *Experience*' (*BB* 383, n. 2).[40]

Watercolour became the usual medium in both Innocence and Experience. In early copies of *Songs of Innocence* and of the combined *Songs*, the edges of the plate were wiped clean of ink so the image appears without a border (or with only a faint trace of one). The colouring is usually simple, with relatively few hues in light, unmodulated washes. Some of the smaller figures (for example in plates 12, 18, 19), and the robes of some larger figures are often uncoloured. The text area is usually left uncoloured too, and where there is no clear separation of text area from image (as in 'The Divine Image', plate 18, figure 8), the entire background may remain uncoloured. Thus the paper tone itself can become a significant element in the visual pattern. In later copies the borders are printed, the impression is coloured to the plate edges, and washes cover the text. The colouring is sometimes elaborate, with a wider range of hues and textures than in the earlier copies. The fine shading in the printed image is often covered over and replaced by colour shading. As Viscomi says 'The contrast between early and late impressions is, generally speaking, between the print-as-page and print-as-painting'.[41] In several of the later copies, linear frames were added around the plates, while two copies – the one reproduced here and copy Y – have elaborate decorative borders.

No general account of Blake's colouring can do justice to its variety: his practice changed from copy to copy, and in this way he continually recreated the work. In some cases there are strong contrasts between fairly dense hues, as in copy R (figure 9); in others the contrasts are gentler, as in copy AA (figure 10). Variations in the colour of individual elements, such as costumes and furnishings, may be determined by purely formal considerations. Some changes may suggest a revised attitude to the text (in early copies the little black boy on plate 10 is usually the same light colour as the little white boy – see figure 11; in later copies he is usually dark). When adding colour Blake often departed from the printed impression by changing details or adding new ones. In copy B, for example, the background of the scene above the text on plate 13 ('The Little Boy lost', figure 12) is simply washed over to create a mist, which obscures the tree etched in vaguely behind the hatless boy. In some copies (e.g. Z and AA) a second tree is added. In most coloured copies the boy is given a hat. Among such local variations a few trends can be identified.[42] On the general title-page of the early copies B–D, Eve faces down-

[40] For a discussion of Blake's experiments with colour printing, see Martin Butlin, 'The Physicality of William Blake: The Large Color Prints of "1795" ', *Huntingdon Library Quarterly*, 52 (1989), 1–17.

[41] *The Art of William Blake's Illuminated Prints*, p. 18.

[42] A detailed account of these variations is given in *BB* 385–404.

wards; in later copies she faces upwards, either towards Adam or ahead. In early copies, the young man on plate 34 is often naked, while the maiden queen on plate 41 is usually without a crown; in later copies he is often clothed, she is usually crowned. Two changes in Blake's practice have a wider effect on the visual appearance of the *Songs*. In later copies streams are often added at the foot of plates 4, 7, 8, 20–1, 23, 47 (and in one or two instances to plates 12, 18, 24, 32, 35, and 49). The streams, which sometimes increase the length of the plate slightly, form a kind of visual boundary between the reader and the scene. Secondly, Blake seems to have become more willing to include haloes in his designs. In early copies the saviour on plate 14 ('The Little Boy found') has a faint, barely distinguishable halo, and the old man who shelters the outcast above the text on plate 45 ('The Little Vagabond') has rays of light about his head – these features were etched on the plates. In later copies other haloes were sometimes added, most often to the saviour figures on plates 10 and 18, and to the females at the foot of plate 21, but occasionally (as in this copy) to other figures as well.

Some of the changes in Blake's practice probably reflect his changing sense of the market for his work. Early copies seem to have been produced with economy in mind. In some (B–F) the plates were printed back-to-back to produce facing pages. Later copies of the *Songs* are more expensively produced – printed on one side of the leaf only, generally on a larger page size. The increase in the price (ten shillings in 1793, six guineas in 1818, ten guineas in 1827) must in part reflect the increased time spent on the colouring, and in some cases perhaps the increased cost of materials.[43] If he devised his own method of printing in the hope of reaching a wider audience, the hope was never realized in his own lifetime. Most of the later copies may have been produced on commission. According to Gilchrist, a copy of the Songs was ordered for ten pounds in 1805, and 'for such a sum Blake could hardly do enough, finishing the plates like miniatures'.[44] Some who commissioned Blake's works may have been more interested in the designs than the text. In a letter of 1818 Blake told Dawson Turner that he had printed a selection from his illuminated books 'without the Writing, tho' with the Loss of some of the best things'.[45] In the same letter he explained that he had printed and sold only a few of his illuminated books, and that these few had gained him 'a great reputation as an Artist, which was the chief thing Intended'. But he can hardly have been satisfied with the limited distribution of his works. The process of production itself proved a limitation, as he realized: 'I have never been able to produce a Sufficient number for a general Sale by means of a regular publisher. It is therefore necessary to me that any Person wishing to have any or all of them should send me their Order to Print them' (*L* 142).

The King's College Copy

Four months before he died, Blake wrote to George Cumberland about his printing activities:

---

[43] *Songs of Innocence* and *Songs of Experience* are priced separately at three guineas each in the letter to Dawson Turner of 9 June 1818 (*L* 142).

[44] Alexander Gilchrist, *Life of William Blake* (London, 1866), p. 60.

[45] This is probably a reference to the two collections of colour printed designs known as the *Large* and *Small Book of Designs*, which are mostly printed from plates of Blake's illuminated books, without the text.

You are desirous I know to dispose of some of my Works & to make them Pleasin[g]. I am obliged to you & to all who do so. But having none remaining of all that I had Printed I cannot Print more Except at a great loss, for at the time I printed those things I had a whole House to range in: now I am shut up in a Corner therefore I am forced to ask a Price for them that I scarce expect to get from a Stranger. I am now Printing a Set of the Songs of Innocence & Experience for a Friend at Ten Guineas which I cannot do under Six Months consistent with my other Work, so that I have little hope of doing any more such things' (*L* 169)

Blake had 'a whole house the range in' during his years at Lambeth (1790–1800), where he would have found the space useful for preparing his printed works. Being 'shut up in a corner' in a two room apartment off the Strand may have made book production difficult, but didn't prevent it. The copy of *Songs* mentioned here was apparently the one ordered by T. G. Wainwright by February 1827 (copy X, see *BR* 339). If 'Six Months' were required to complete a copy, Blake would not have had time to produce any more before he died (on 12 August 1827). But in that case his claim to have 'none remaining of all that I had Printed' is puzzling, perhaps misleading.[46] The copy of the *Songs* reproduced in this edition cannot have been printed before 1825, as the watermarks indicate.[47] It must have been among the stock of works unsold at Blake's death, a stock that supplied an important source of income for his widow.

PRINTING AND COLOURING

Whether or not Blake had a customer in mind when he produced this copy, he seems to have spared no expense on it, either of time or materials. It had become his usual practice to print on one side of the leaf only, but the size of the leaves here is relatively generous (about 28 cm × 22 cm).[48] The basic image on each plate was printed in light red-brown ink, which usually blends in easily with the hues of foliage or bark, with fleece and flesh tones, or with the costumes. Sometimes it contrasts with the dominant impression of the plate – as when it adds warmth to the snow scene of 'The Chimney Sweeper' in Experience (37). In the first plate of 'Night' (20) the print colour is almost entirely overpainted with a pale yellow ochre, creating a soft, cool atmosphere. Often some details of the original printed image are obscure, either because overpainted or because the original impression was faint. In places Blake was content to leave details vague, as in the tiny vignettes on plate 4 (the 'Introduction' to Innocence). But facial expressions are usually picked out in ink, while the outlines of figures and costumes, tree trunks and branches, stems and petals may be carefully reinforced in black or grey. Blake generally gives more attention to the design than to the text, which is often unevenly printed and sometimes difficult to read. His treatment of the text is oddly inconsistent – in some places it is carefully retouched, in others it is left faint and blurred. The same poem may exhibit both care and apparent neglect. In most cases, though, the text remains legible.

The colouring of the plates is particularly rich. Blake worked with a relatively full pallette, and achieved considerable variety in texture and effects of light. The text area

---

46 Although Blake preferred to work to commission, he evidently did produce copies of his own works without having a customer for them (as his reference to the 'Finish'd' copy of *Jerusalem* in the same letter indicates).

47 Fifteen leaves are watermarked: 'J Whatman 1818' appears on plate 15; 'J Whatman 1825' is visible on plates 11, 17, 20, 22, 27, 30, 31, 33, 35, 42, 43, 44, 49, 54.

48 Copies A, R, V and X are also printed on large leaves. The book is usually printed on leaves measuring about 20 × 14 cm. The leaves in this copy have been trimmed and gilt.

is often washed to become part of a sky in which pale blues, yellows and pinks blend together, darkening to purple and grey. Against the translucent washes, foliage and costumes may have a more opaque colouring, sometimes layered to give density, sometimes combining pigments in subtle modulations. Rose and purple madder combine to create the red costumes that recur in both series, sometimes heightened with crimson – as in the dress of the Maiden Queen on plate 41. The blue costumes sometimes use comparable combinations. One of the most striking features of this copy is the abundance of gold, which appears in varying densities. Presumably Blake used 'shell gold' (gold leaf ground to powder and mixed like other pigments in water and a fixative), applying it with a brush to produce the light granular washes that shade costumes, grass, fleece and hair, and that occasionally brighten the skies.[49] In places it is very faint, visible only in an oblique light. It appears more densely in the song titles, in fine rays from haloes, in highlights flecking trees or touching the stems and tendrils of vines. Sometimes the text has been retouched in gold (plates 20 and 25). The edges of some plates are partially lined with it.

A concern with harmony and balance in the colouring can be seen throughout the volume. Where there are groups of figures, as in plates 6–7 ('The Ecchoing Green'), 15 ('Laughing Song') or 54 ('The Voice of the Ancient Bard'), costume colours are distributed for variety and loose symmetry. Colour densities are varied to achieve a comparable effect, as in plate 34 ('The Little Girl Lost'). The shape of the plate is often emphasized by darker tones at the edges, by the green earth at the foot of the plate (sometimes with water), and occasionally by foliage added in the upper corners as in plates 11 ('The Blossom') and 51 ('A Little Girl Lost').

The contribution of the colouring to the significance of the designs is usually obvious, and entirely dependent on context. 'Warm' colours may suggest joyful exuberance, as in the brilliant crimson of the flower in 'Infant Joy', or they may indicate the repression of desire, as in the glowing red costume of the Maiden Queen in 'The Angel'. The blue costume of the piper on plate 2 (the Innocence frontispiece) blends with the cool shades of the pastoral setting to give a sense of concord between the youth and his environment; the blue costume of the mother on plate 17 ('Cradle Song') may associate her with the Madonna. The young boy whose hair is combed so carefully on plate 38 (the Experience 'Nurses Song') has gold shading over his costume and hair – which seems to confirm the impression of vanity created by his pose. The naked boy who warms himself in the margin of plate 46 ('London') is also golden – but seems as remote from vanity as the golden angels that guard the margins of some Innocence plates. In the stylized images that illustrate 'The Blossom' (plate 11) and 'The Divine Image' (plate 18) colour is used emblematically to suggest a harmonizing of opposites.

THE DECORATIVE BORDERS

According to a letter written by Laura Mary Forster (see appendix), George Richmond claimed that the decorative borders in this copy were added by Catherine Blake after her husband's death. As it stands this claim seems dubious. In some cases (e.g. plates 31 and 54) the borders break into the plate area, and as there is no sign of revision here, it

---

[49] The preparation of 'shell gold' from gold leaf is described in detail by Robert Dossie, *The Handmaid to the Arts* (London, 1764), pp. 445–6.

is hard to see how they can have been added after the rest of the plate was coloured: they are an integral part of the composition. Catherine Blake certainly helped Blake to print some of his works (see *L* 52) and according to Frederick Tatham she 'was no small use in the completion of his laborious designs' (*BR* 534). She may have helped in the production of his illuminated works, including this one. But apart from the questionable evidence of the letter there is no reason to think that the borders, with their delicate brushwork and their Blakean motifs, were not devised and executed by Blake himself.[50] Outside the borders he numbered each plate in orange at the top right corner (except plate 2, which is numbered in pencil in a different hand).

The borders are usually coloured in light brown, pale Prussian green, black (along the base), with some pink and, occasionally, gold. Some decorations form a complete frame, others spring directly from the edges of the plate. Many seem purely decorative, like the simple rectangular frames around the Innocence 'Nurse's Song', or 'London'. Others are clearly related to elements in the design or to the mood of the song. The snow scene on plate 37 has a snowy border. Curtains frame 'A Cradle Song', 'A Dream', and – echoing the drapery in the design – 'Infant Sorrow'. Sometimes the relationship is more suggestive. The rams' heads at the top of plate 31 ('Earth's Answer') are images of sacrifice that illuminate Earth's protest against 'Cruel jealous selfish fear'. The vine, with or without a supporting trellis, is the most common motif, and is perhaps an emblem of Christ's eternal presence in both states of the soul.

PROVENANCE

According to entries in John Linnell's Journal, Catherine Blake sold this copy of the *Songs* to John Jebb, Bishop of Limerick, in 1830. The entry for 25 February notes that Haviland Burke called on Linnell to find out how the Bishop 'could best serve Mrs Blake'. Linnell advised Burke 'to recommend to the Bishop to purchase the works of Mr. Bl *from Mrs. B.*'. On 3 March Linnell 'Went with Mr H. Burke to Mrs Blake & selected two drawings 8gs – two prints of Job & Ezekiel, 2 gs. – & the coloured copy of Songs of Innocence & Experience, making 20 gs. – which the Bishop of Limerick sent Mr Burke to lay out with Mrs Blake' (*BR* 379). The copy was thus sold for 10 guineas, the price Blake had mentioned in 1827. Linnell's account of the sale conflicts with, and seems to disprove, that given by Gilchrist in his *Life of Blake*. Gilchrist says Mrs Blake gave it to Jebb in gratitude for a gift of 20 guineas sent after Blake's death: the copy was 'in her estimation especially precious for having been "Blake's own" ' (p. 365). But there seems no reason to doubt Linnell.

When the Bishop died in 1833, the volume passed to his curate Charles Forster, who left it to Laura Mary Forster, his eldest daughter. Her bookplate appears on a flyleaf, and she inserted a hand written record of the volume's descent from Jebb to her father and to herself, signed and dated 27 June 1903.[51] On 1 January 1904 she gave the volume to

[50] As Richmond 'did not like all of the decorations' he may have wanted to dissociate them from Blake. There seems to be no other evidence to support this view.

[51] By this time the volume had been rebound in red morocco (with stab holes at intervals of about 0.9 cms). The documents relating to the provenance of the copy were attached to the inside leaves of the binding. The volume was originally bound through three stab holes (at about 9.2 cm from the top, then at intervals of 4.3 cm and 4.5 cm). At the time of writing it is unbound.

her nephew, E. M. Forster.[52] It remained in the novelist's possession for the next fifty-five years, although by 1939 he had willed it to King's College, Cambridge (according to a note with the volume, signed by him and dated September 8, 1939). On 7 January 1959 he wrote to the College Librarian (then Dr A. N. L. Munby) offering the volume to the College to mark his eightieth birthday. This note is also included in the volume. As Keynes says in his discussion of this history, 'the facts establish that the book has never been sold at auction'.[53] During the last 160 years few have been able to see it. In this present edition, it should at last begin to reach a wider audience.

[52] On 14 May 1923 Laura Forster wrote to her nephew assuring him that Gilchrist's account of how the Bishop acquired the volume is 'the true version' (part of the letter is included in the volume: see appendix). Gilchrists's account had been challenged by A. T. Storey in *The Life of John Linnell* (1892), pp. 243–4.

[53] Geoffrey Keynes, ' "Blake's Own" Copy of Songs of Innocence and of Experience', *Book Collector* 29 (1980), 202–7 (p. 206).

The Plates
with a transcription of the text

A Note on the Text

BLAKE's process of illuminated printing frequently transforms the punctuation etched on the plates: commas become full stops, semicolons become colons, etc. Blake rarely corrected such accidents of the press. In reproducing the text of this copy in conventional typography I have attempted to preserve its erratic punctuation as far as possible. The attempt involves some arbitrary decisions, as indeterminate marks must be transformed into definite stops. Marks that are low relative to the print line, or elongated vertically, or have hints of tails, are transcribed as commas (or create semicolons) except where they terminate sentences. Readers will soon find that commas, full stops, semicolons and colons are sometimes used in the text as if interchangeable, and seem to function as pauses rather than as guides to sentence structure. I have ignored the distinction in Blake's text between italic and upright miniscule roman lettering, except where both are used in one poem (plate 51). Catchwords are italicized.

1

Combined Title-page

2

[Innocence Frontispiece]

3

Innocence Title-page

Introduction

Piping down the valleys wild
Piping songs of pleasant glee
On a cloud I saw a child.
And he laughing said to me.

Pipe a song about a Lamb:
So I piped with merry chear,
Piper pipe that song again—
So I piped, he wept to hear.

Drop thy pipe thy happy pipe
Sing thy songs of happy chear,
So I sung the same again
While he wept with joy to hear

Piper sit thee down and write
In a book that all may read—
So he vanish'd from my sight
And I pluck'd a hollow reed

And I made a rural pen,
And I stain'd the water clear,
And I wrote my happy songs,
Every child may joy to hear.

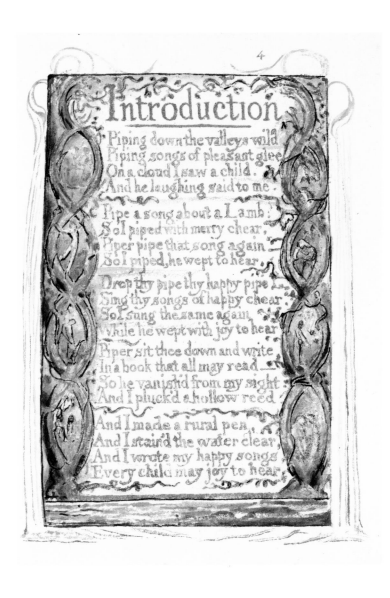

Introduction

Piping down the valleys wild
Piping songs of pleasant glee
On a cloud I saw a child.
And he laughing said to me.

Pipe a song about a Lamb:
So I piped with merry chear,
Piper pipe that song again—
So I piped, he wept to hear.

Drop thy pipe thy happy pipe
Sing thy songs of happy chear,
So I sung the same again
While he wept with joy to hear

Piper sit thee down and write
In a book that all may read—
So he vanish'd from my sight.
And I pluck'd a hollow reed

And I made a rural pen,
And I stain'd the water clear,
And I wrote my happy songs
Every child may joy to hear

5

The Shepherd.

How sweet is the Shepherds sweet lot,
From the morn to the evening he strays:
He shall follow his sheep all the day
And his tongue shall be filled with praise.

For he hears the lambs innocent call.
And he hears the ewes tender reply,
He is watchful while they are in peace,
For they know when their Shepherd is nigh.

6

The Ecchoing Green

The Sun does arise,
And make happy the skies.
The merry bells ring,
To welcome the Spring.
The sky-lark and thrush,
The birds of the bush,
Sing louder around,
To the bells chearful sound.
While our sports shall be seen
On the Ecchoing Green.

Old John with white hair
Does laugh away care,
Sitting under the oak,
Among the old folk.

They

The Ecchoing Green

The Sun does arise,
And make happy the skies;
The merry bells ring,
To welcome the Spring.
The sky-lark and thrush,
The birds of the bush,
Sing louder around,
To the bells chearful sound,
While our sports shall be seen
On the Ecchoing Green.

Old John with white hair
Does laugh away care,
Sitting under the oak,
Among the old folk.
They

7

They laugh at our play,
And soon they all say,
Such such were the joys.
When we all girls & boys.
In our youth time were seen,
On the Ecchoing Green.

Till the little ones weary
No more can be merry
The sun does descend,
And our sports have an end:
Round the laps of their mothers.
Many sisters and brothers,
Like birds in their nest.
Are ready for rest;
And sport no more seen,
On the darkening Green.

8

The Lamb

Little Lamb who made thee
Dost thou know who made thee
Gave thee life & bid thee feed.
By the stream & o'er the mead;
Gave thee clothing of delight.
Softest clothing wooly bright;
Gave thee such a tender voice.
Making all the vales rejoice:
Little Lamb who made thee
Dost thou know who made thee

Little Lamb I'll tell thee,
Little Lamb Ill tell thee;
He is called by thy name,
For he calls himself a Lamb:
He is meek & he is mild,
He became a little child:
I a child & thou a lamb,
We are called by his name,
Little Lamb God bless thee,
Little Lamb God bless thee.

9

The Little Black Boy

My mother bore me in the southern wild,
And I am black, but O! my soul is white.
White as an angel is the English child:
But I am black as if bereav'd of light.

My mother taught me underneath a tree
And sitting down before the heat of day.
She took me on her lap and kissed me,
And pointing to the east began to say.

Look on the rising sun: there God does live
And gives his light. and gives his heat away.
And flowers and trees and beasts and men recieve
Comfort in morning joy in the noon day.

And we are put on earth a little space..
That we may learn to bear the beams of love.
And these black bodies and this sun-burnt face
Is but a cloud, and like a shady grove.

For

The Little Black Boy

My mother bore me in the southern wild,
And I am black, but O! my soul is white.
White as an angel is the English child:
But I am black as if bereav'd of light.

My mother taught me underneath a tree
And sitting down before the heat of day
She took me on her lap and kissed me,
And pointing to the east began to say.

Look on the rising sun: there God does live
And gives his light, and gives his heat away.
And flowers and trees and beasts and men recieve
Comfort in morning joy in the noon day.

And we are put on earth a little space,
That we may learn to bear the beams of love.
And these black bodies and this sunburnt face
Is but a cloud, and like a shady grove.

For

10

For when our souls have learn'd the heat to bear
The cloud will vanish we shall hear his voice.
Saying: come out from the grove my love & care.
And round my golden tent like lambs rejoice.

Thus did my mother say and kissed me.
And thus I say to little English boy.
When I from black and he from white cloud free,
And round the tent of God like lambs we joy:

Ill shade him from the heat till he can bear,
To lean in joy upon our fathers knee.
And then I'll stand and stroke his silver hair,
And be like him and he will then love me.

For when our souls have learn'd the heat to bear
The cloud will vanish we shall hear his voice.
Saying: come out from the grove my love & care.
And round my golden tent like lambs rejoice.

Thus did my mother say and kissed me,
And thus I say to little English boy.
When I from black and he from white cloud free,
And round the tent of God like lambs we joy:

Ill shade him from the heat till he can bear,
To lean in joy upon our fathers knee.
And then I'll stand and stroke his silver hair,
And be like him and he will then love me.

11

The Blossom.

Merry Merry Sparrow
Under leaves so green
A happy Blossom
Sees you swift as arrow
Seek your cradle narrow
Near my Bosom.

Pretty Pretty Robin
Under leaves so green
A happy Blossom
Hears you sobbing sobbing
Pretty Pretty Robin
Near my Bosom.

The Blossom.

Merry Merry Sparrow
Under leaves so green
A happy Blossom
Sees you swift as arrow
Seek your cradle narrow
Near my Bosom.

Pretty Pretty Robin
Under leaves so green
A happy Blossom
Hears you sobbing sobbing
Pretty Pretty Robin
Near my Bosom.

12

The Chimney Sweeper

When my mother died I was very young,
And my father sold me while yet my tongue,
Could scarcely cry weep weep weep weep,
So your chimneys I sweep & in soot I sleep.

Theres little Tom Dacre. who cried when his head
That curl'd like a lambs back, was shav'd, so I said.
Hush Tom never mind it, for when your head's bare,
You know that the soot cannot spoil your white hair

And so he was quiet. & that very night.
As Tom was a sleeping he had such a sight,
That thousands of sweepers Dick, Joe, Ned & Jack
Were all of them lock'd up in coffins of black,

And by came an Angel who had a bright key
And he open'd the coffins & set them all free.
Then down a green plain leaping laughing they run
And wash in a river and shine in the Sun.

Then naked & white, all their bags left behind.
They rise upon clouds, and sport in the wind.
And the Angel told Tom, if he'd be a good boy,
He'd have God for his father & never want joy.

And so Tom awoke and we rose in the dark
And got with our bags & our brushes to work.
Tho' the morning was cold, Tom was happy & warm
So if all do their duty, they need not fear harm.

The Chimney Sweeper

When my mother died I was very young,
And my father sold me while yet my tongue,
Could scarcely cry weep weep weep weep.
So your chimneys I sweep & in soot I sleep.

Theres little Tom Dacre, who cried when his head
That curld like a lambs back, was shav'd, so I said.
Hush Tom never mind it, for when your heads bare,
You know that the soot cannot spoil your white hair.

And so he was quiet, & that very night,
As Tom was a sleeping he had such a sight,
That thousands of sweepers Dick, Joe, Ned & Jack
Were all of them lock'd up in coffins of black,

And by came an Angel who had a bright key,
And he open'd the coffins & set them all free.
Then down a green plain leaping laughing they run
And wash in a river and shine in the Sun.

Then naked & white, all their bags left behind,
They rise upon clouds, and sport in the wind.
And the Angel told Tom if he'd be a good boy,
He'd have God for his father & never want joy.

And so Tom awoke and we rose in the dark
And got with our bags & our brushes to work.
Tho' the morning was cold, Tom was happy & warm,
So if all do their duty, they need not fear harm.

13

The Little Boy lost

Father, father, where are you going
O do not walk so fast.
Speak father, speak to your little boy
Or else I shall be lost,

The night was dark no father was there
The child was wet with dew.
The mire was deep, & the child did weep
And away the vapour flew

The Little Boy lost

Father. father. where are you going
O do not walk so fast.
Speak father, speak to your little boy
Or else I shall be lost.

The night was dark no father was there
The child was wet with dew.
The mire was deep. & the child did weep
And away the vapour flew.

14

The Little Boy found

The little boy lost in the lonely fen,
Led by the wand'ring light,
Began to cry, but God ever nigh,
Appeard like his father in white.

He kissed the child & by the hand led
And to his mother brought,
Who in sorrow pale. thro' the lonely dale
Her little boy weeping sought.

The Little Boy found

The little boy lost in the lonely fen,
Led by the wand'ring light,
Began to cry, but God ever nigh,
Appeard like his father in white.

He kissed the child & by the hand led
And to his mother brought,
Who in sorrow pale, thro' the lonely dale
Her little boy weeping sought.

15

Laughing Song,

When the green woods laugh with the voice of joy
And the dimpling stream runs laughing by,
When the air does laugh with our merry wit,
And the green hill laughs with the noise of it.

When the meadows laugh with lively green
And the grasshopper laughs in the merry scene.
When Mary and Susan and Emily.
With their sweet round mouths sing Ha, Ha, He.

When the painted birds laugh in the shade
Where our table with cherries and nuts is spre[ad]
Come live & be merry and join with me,
To sing the sweet chorus of Ha, Ha, He.

Laughing Song

When the green woods laugh with the voice of joy
And the dimpling stream runs laughing by,
When the air does laugh with our merry wit,
And the green hill laughs with the noise of it.

When the meadows laugh with lively green
And the grasshopper laughs in the merry scene,
When Mary and Susan and Emily.
With their sweet round mouths sing Ha Ha He.

When the painted birds laugh in the shade
Where our table with cherries and nuts is spread
Come live & be merry and join with me,
To sing the sweet chorus of Ha Ha He.

16

A CRADLE SONG

Sweet dreams form a shade,
O'er my lovely infants head.
Sweet dreams of pleasant streams,
By happy silent moony beams

Sweet sleep with soft down.
Weave thy brows an infant crown.
Sweet sleep Angel mild,
Hover o'er my happy child.

Sweet smiles in the night,
Hover over my delight.
Sweet smiles Mothers smiles
All the livelong night beguiles.

Sweet moans, dovelike sighs,
Chase not slumber from thy eyes,
Sweet moans. sweeter smiles,
All the dovelike moans beguiles.

Sleep sleep happy child,
All creation slept and smil'd.
Sleep sleep, happy sleep.
While o'er thee thy mother weep

Sweet babe in thy face,
Holy image I can trace.
Sweet babe once like thee.
Thy maker lay and wept for me

Wept

A CRADLE SONG

Sweet dreams form a shade,
O'er my lovely infants head.
Sweet dreams of pleasant streams,
By happy silent moony beams

Sweet sleep with soft down,
Weave thy brows an infant crown.
Sweet sleep Angel mild,
Hover o'er my happy child.

Sweet smiles in the night,
Hover over my delight.
Sweet smiles Mothers smiles
All the livelong night beguiles.

Sweet moans, dovelike sighs,
Chase not slumber from thy eyes.
Sweet moans, sweeter smiles,
All the dovelike moans beguiles.

Sleep sleep happy child.
All creation slept and smil'd.
Sleep sleep, happy sleep.
While o'er thee thy mother weep

Sweet babe in thy face.
Holy image I can trace.
Sweet babe once like thee.
Thy maker lay and wept for me

Wept

17

Wept for me for thee for all,
When he was an infant small.
Thou his image ever see.
Heavenly face that smiles on thee,

Smiles on thee on me on all,
Who became an infant small,
Infant smiles are his own smiles,
Heaven & earth to peace beguiles.

Wept for me for thee for all,
When he was an infant small.
Thou his image ever see.
Heavenly face that smiles on thee,

Smiles on thee on me on all
Who became an infant small.
Infant smiles are his own smiles,
Heaven & earth to peace beguiles

18

The Divine Image.

To Mercy Pity Peace and Love.
All pray in their distress:
And to these virtues of delight
Return their thankfulness.

For Mercy Pity Peace and Love,
Is God our father dear:
And Mercy Pity Peace and Love,
Is Man his child and care.

For Mercy has a human heart
Pity, a human face:
And Love, the human form divine,
And Peace, the human dress.

Then every man of every clime,
That prays in his distress,
Prays to the human form divine
Love Mercy Pity Peace,

And all must love the human form.
In heathen, turk or jew,
Where Mercy, Love & Pity dwell,
There God is dwelling too.

The Divine Image.

To Mercy Pity Peace and Love,
All pray in their distress:
And to these virtues of delight
Return their thankfulness.

For Mercy Pity Peace and Love,
Is God our father dear:
And Mercy Pity Peace and Love,
Is Man his child and care.

For Mercy has a human heart
Pity, a human face:
And Love, the human form divine,
And Peace, the human dress.

Then every man of every clime,
That prays in his distress,
Prays to the human form divine
Love Mercy Pity Peace.

And all must love the human form,
In heathen, turk or jew,
Where Mercy, Love & Pity dwell,
There God is dwelling too.

HOLY THURSDAY

Twas on a Holy Thursday their innocent faces clean
The children walking two & two in red & blue & gre[en]
Grey headed beadles walkd before with wands as white as snow
Till into the high dome of Pauls they like Thames waters flow

O what a multitude they seemd these flowers of London town
Seated in companies they sit with radiance all their own
The hum of multitudes was there but multitudes of lambs
Thousands of little boys & girls raising their innocent hands

Now like a mighty wind they raise to heaven the voice of song
Or like harmonious thunderings the seats of heaven among
Beneath them sit the aged men wise guardians of the poor
Then cherish pity, lest you drive an angel from your door

HOLY THURSDAY

Twas on a Holy Thursday their innocent faces clean
The children walking two & two in red & blue & green
Grey headed beadles walkd before with wands as white as snow
Till into the high dome of Pauls they like Thames waters flow

O what a multitude they seemd these flowers of London town
Seated in companies they sit with radiance all their own
The hum of multitudes was there but multitudes of lambs
Thousands of little boys & girls raising their innocent hands

Now like a mighty wind they raise to heaven the voice of song
Or like harmonious thunderings the seats of heaven among
Beneath them sit the aged men wise guardians of the poor
Then cherish pity. lest you drive an angel from your door

20

Night

The sun descending in the west.
The evening star does shine.
The birds are silent in their nest,
And I must seek for mine,
The moon like a flower,
In heavens high bower;
With silent delight,
Sits and smiles on the night.

Farewell green fields and happy groves,
Where flocks have took delight;
Where lambs have nibbled, silent moves
The feet of angels bright;
Unseen they pour blessing,
And joy without ceasing,
On each bud and blossom,
And each sleeping bosom.

They look in every thoughtless nest
Where birds are coverd warm;
They visit caves of every beast,
To keep them all from harm;
If they see any weeping,
That should have been sleeping
They pour sleep on their head
And sit down by their bed.

[*When*]

Night

The sun descending in the west,
The evening star does shine,
The birds are silent in their nest,
And I must seek for mine,
The moon like a flower,
In heavens high bower,
With silent delight,
Sits and smiles on the night.

Farewell green fields and happy groves,
Where flocks have took delight;
Where lambs have nibbled, silent moves
The feet of angels bright;
Unseen they pour blessing,
And joy without ceasing,
On each bud and blossom,
And each sleeping bosom

They look in every thoughtless nest,
Where birds are cover'd warm;
They visit caves of every beast,
To keep them all from harm,
If they see any weeping,
That should have been sleeping
They pour sleep on their head
And sit down by their bed.

When wolves and tygers howl for prey
They pitying stand and weep;
Seeking to drive their thirst away,
And keep them from the sheep.
But if they rush dreadful;
The angels most heedful,
Recieve each mild spirit.
New worlds to inherit.

And there the lions ruddy eyes,
Shall flow with tears of gold;
And pitying the tender cries,
And walking round the fold:
Saying: wrath by his meekness
And by his health, sickness.
Is driven away,
From our immortal day.

And now beside thee bleating lamb.
I can lie down and sleep;
Or think on him who bore thy name.
Grase after thee and weep.
For wash'd in lifes river.
My bright mane for ever.
Shall shine like the gold.
As I guard o'er the fold.

When wolves and tygers howl for prey
They pitying stand and weep;
Seeking to drive their thirst away
And keep them from the sheep.
But if they rush dreadful;
The angels most heedful,
Recieve each mild spirit
New worlds to inherit.

And there the lions ruddy eyes,
Shall flow with tears of gold:
And pitying the tender cries,
And walking round the fold:
Saying: wrath by his meekness,
And by his health, sickness
Is driven away,
From our immortal day.

And now beside thee bleating lamb,
I can lie down and sleep;
Or think on him who bore thy name
Graze after thee and weep.
For washd in lifes river,
My bright mane for ever,
Shall shine like the gold,
As I guard o'er the fold.

22

Spring

Sound the Flute!
Now it's mute.
Birds delight
Day and Night,
Nightingale
In the dale
Lark in Sky
Merrily
Merrily Merrily to welcome in the Year

Little Boy
Full of joy,

Little

Spring

Sound the Flute!
Now it's mute.
Birds delight
Day and Night.
Nightingale
In the dale
Lark in Sky
Merrily   (Year
Merrily Merrily to welcome in the

Little Boy
Full of joy.   Little

23

Little Girl
Sweet and small,
Cock does crow
So do you.
Merry voice
Infant noise
Merrily Merrily to welcome in the Year

Little Lamb
Here I am.
Come and lick
My white neck.
Let me pull
Your soft Wool.
Let me kiss
Your soft face
Merrily Merrily we welcome in the Year

Little Girl
Sweet and small
Cock does crow
So do you,
Merry voice
Infant noise
Merrily Merrily to welcome in the Year

Little Lamb
Here I am
Come and lick
My white neck
Let me pull
Your soft Wool.
Let me kiss
Your soft face
Merrily Merrily we welcome in the   Year

24

Nurse's Song

When the voices of children are heard on the green
And laughing is heard on the hill,
My heart is at rest within my breast
And everything else is still

Then come home my children the sun is gone down
And the dews of night arise
Come come leave off play, and let us away ·
Till the morning appears in the skies

No no let us play, for it is yet day
And we cannot go to sleep
Besides in the sky, the little birds fly
And the hills are all coverd with sheep

Well well go & play till the light fades away
And then go home to bed
The little ones leaped & shouted & laugh'd
And all the hills ecchoed

Nurses Song

When the voices of children are heard on the green
And laughing is heard on the hill,
My heart is at rest within my breast
And every thing else is still

Then come home my children the sun is gone down
And the dews of night arise
Come come leave off play, and let us away
Till the morning appears in the skies

No no let us play, for it is yet day
And we cannot go to sleep
Besides in the sky, the little birds fly
And the hills are all coverd with sheep

Well well go & play till the light fades away
And then go home to bed
The little ones leaped & shouted & laughd
And all the hills ecchoed

Infant Joy

I have no name
I am but two days old.—
What shall I call thee?
I happy am
Joy is my name.—
Sweey joy befall thee!

Pretty joy!
Sweet joy but two days old.
Sweet joy I call thee;
Thou dost smile,
I sing the while
Sweet joy befall thee.

Infant Joy

I have no name
I am but two days old.—
What shall I call thee?
I happy am
Joy is my name.—
Sweet joy befall thee!

Pretty joy!
Sweet joy but two days old.
Sweet joy I call thee:
Thou dost smile.
I sing the while
Sweet joy befall thee.

A Dream

Once a dream did weave a shade,
O'er my Angel-guarded bed.
That an Emmet lost it's way
Where on grass methought I lay.

Troubled wilderd and forlorn
Dark benighted travel-worn,
Over many a tangled spray,
All heart-broke I heard her say.

O my children! do they cry,
Do they hear their father sigh.
Now they look abroad to see,
Now return and weep for me.

Pitying I drop'd a tear;
But I saw a glow-worm near:
Who replied. What wailing wight
Calls the watchman of the night.

I am set to light the ground,
While the beetle goes his round:
Follow now the beetles hum,
Little wanderer hie thee home.

A Dream

Once a dream did weave a shade,
O'er my Angel-guarded bed,
That an Emmet lost it's way
Where on grass methought I lay.

Troubled wilderd and folorn
Dark benighted travel-worn,
Over many a tangled spray,
All heart-broke I heard her say.

O my children! do they cry,
Do they hear their father sigh.
Now they look abroad to see,
Now return and weep for me.

Pitying I dropd a tear:
But I saw a glow-worm near:
Who replied. What wailing wight
Calls the watchman of the night.

I am set to light the ground,
While the beetle goes his round:
Follow now the beetles hum,
Little wanderer hie thee home.

27

On Anothers Sorrow

Can I see anothers woe,
And not be in sorrow too.
Can I see anothers grief,
And not seek for kind relief.

Can I see a falling tear.
And not feel my sorrows share,
Can a father see his child,
Weep, nor be with sorrow fill'd.

Can a mother sit and hear.
An infant groan an infant fear—
No no never can it be,
Never never can it be.

And can he who smiles on all
Hear the wren with sorrows small.
Hear the small birds grief & care
Hear the woes that infants bear—

And not sit beside the nest
Pouring pity in their breast.
And not sit the cradle near
Weeping tear on infants tear.

And not sit both night & day.
Wiping all our tears away.
O! no never can it be.
Never never can it be.

He doth give his joy to all,
He becomes an infant small,
He becomes a man of woe
He doth feel the sorrow too.

Think not. thou canst sigh a sigh,
And thy maker is not by.
Think not, thou canst weep a tear,
And thy maker is not near.

O! he gives to us his joy.
That our grief he may destroy
Till our grief is fled & gone
He doth sit by us and moan

On Anothers Sorrow

Can I see anothers woe,
And not be in sorrow too.
Can I see anothers grief,
And not seek for kind relief.

Can I see a falling tear,
And not feel my sorrows share,
Can a father see his child,
Weep, nor be with sorrow filld.

Can a mother sit and hear,
An infant groan an infant fear—
No no never can it be.
Never never can it be.

And can he who smiles on all
Hear the wren with sorrows small,
Hear the small birds grief & care
Hear the woes that infants bear—

And not sit beside the nest
Pouring pity in their breast.
And not sit the cradle near
Weeping tear on infants tear.

And not sit both night & day,
Wiping all our tears away.
O! no never can it be.
Never never can it be.

He doth give his joy to all.
He becomes an infant small.
He becomes a man of woe
He doth feel the sorrow too.

Think not thou canst sigh a sigh,
And thy maker is not by.
Think not thou canst weep a tear,
And thy maker is not near.

O! he gives to us his joy.
That our grief he may destroy
Till our grief is fled & gone
He doth sit by us and moan

28

[Experience Frontispiece]

29

Experience Title-page

Introduction.

Hear the voice of the Bard!
Who Present, Past, & Future sees
Whose ears have heard,
The Holy Word,
That walk'd among the ancient trees.

Calling the lapsed Soul
And weeping in the evening dew;
That might controll.
The starry pole;
And fallen fallen light renew!

O Earth O Earth return!
Arise from out the dewy grass;
Night is worn,
And the morn
Rises from the slumberous mass.

Turn away no more:
Why wilt thou turn away
The starry floor
The watry shore
Is givn thee till the break of day.

Introduction.

Hear the voice of the Bard!
Who Present, Past, & Future sees
Whose ears have heard,
The Holy Word,
That walk'd among the ancient trees.

Calling the lapsed Soul,
And weeping in the evening dew:
That might controll.
The starry pole;
And fallen fallen light renew!

O Earth O Earth return!
Arise from out the dewy grass;
Night is worn,
And the morn
Rises from the slumberous mals.

Turn away no more:
Why wilt thou turn away
The starry floor
The watry shore
Is given thee till the break of day.

EARTH'S Answer

Earth raisd up her head.
From the darkness dread & drear.
Her light fled:
Stony dread!
And her locks cover'd with grey despair.

Prison'd on watry shore
Starry Jealousy does keep my den
Cold and hoar
Weeping o'er
I hear the father of the ancient men

Selfish father of men
Cruel jealous selfish fear
Can delight
Chain'd in night
The virgins of youth and morning bear.

Does spring hide its joy
When buds and blossoms grow?
Does the sower?
Sow by night?
Or the plowman in darkness plow?

Break this heavy chain.
That does freeze my bones around
Selfish! vain!
Eternal bane!
That free Love with bondage bound.

EARTH'S *Answer*

Earth raisd up her head,
From the darkness dread & drear,
Her light fled:
Stony dread!
And her locks cover'd with grey despair.

Prison'd on watry shore
Starry Jealousy does keep my den
Cold and hoar
Weeping o'er
I hear the father of the ancient men

Selfish father of men
Cruel jealous selfish fear
Can delight
Chain'd in night
The virgins of youth and morning bear.

Does spring hide its joy
When buds and blossoms grow?
Does the sower?
Sow by night?
Or the plowman in darkness plow?

Break this heavy chain,
That does freeze my bones around
Selfish! vain!
Eternal bane!
That free Love with bondage bound.

The CLOD & the PEBBLE

Love seeketh not Itself to please.
Nor for itself hath any care;
But for another gives its ease.
And builds a Heaven in Hells despair.

    So sung a little Clod of Clay,
    Trodden with the cattles feet;
    But a Pebble of the brook.
    Warbled out these metres meet.

Love seeketh only Self to please,
To bind another to Its delight;
Joys in anothers loss of ease.
And builds a Hell in Heavens despite.

The CLOD & the PEBBLE

Love seeketh not Itself to please,
Nor for itself hath any care;
But for another gives its ease,
And builds a Heaven in Hells despair.

So sung a little Clod of Clay,
Trodden with the cattles feet:
But a Pebble of the brook,
Warbled out these metres meet.

Love seeketh only Self to please,
To bind another to Its delight:
Joys in anothers loss of ease,
And builds a Hell in Heavens despite.

HOLY THURSDAY

Is this a holy thing to see.
In a rich and fruitful land.
Babes reducd to misery.
Fed with cold and usurous hand?

Is that trembling cry a song?
Can it be a song of joy?
And so many children poor?
It is a land of poverty!

And their sun does never shine.
And their fields are bleak & bare.
And their ways are fill'd with thorns
It is eternal winter there.

For where-e'er the sun does shine.
And where-e'er the rain does fall:
Babe can never hunger there,
Nor poverty the mind appall.

HOLY THURSDAY

Is this a holy thing to see,
In a rich and fruitful land,
Babes reduced to misery,
Fed with cold and usurous hand?

Is that trembling cry a song?
Can it be a song of joy?
And so many children poor?
It is a land of poverty!

And their sun does never shine,
And their fields are bleak & bare,
And their ways are fill'd with thorns
It is eternal winter there.

For where-eer the sun does shine,
And where-eer the rain does fall:
Babe can never hunger there,
Nor poverty the mind appall.

The Little Girl Lost

In futurity
I prophetic see.
That the earth from sleep.
(Grave the sentence deep)

Shall arise and seek
For her maker meek:
And the desart wild
Become a garden mild.

In the southern clime,
Where the summers prime.
Never fades away;
Lovely Lyca lay.

Seven summers old
Lovely Lyca told,
She had wanderd long.
Hearing wild birds song.

Sweet sleep come to me
Underneath this tree;
Do father, mother weep.—
"Where can Lyca sleep".

Lost in desart wild
Is your little child.
How can Lyca sleep.
If her mother weep.

If her heart does ake.
Then let Lyca wake;
If my mother sleep,
Lyca shall not weep.

Frowning frowning night,
O'er this desart bright.
Let thy moon arise.
While I close my eyes.

Sleeping Lyca lay:
While the beasts of prey,
Come from caverns deep,
View'd the maid asleep

The kingly lion stood
And the virgin view'd,
Then he gambold round
O'er the hallowd ground:

Leo[pard]s

The Little Girl Lost.

In futurity
I prophetic see,
That the earth from sleep.
(Grave the sentence deep)

Shall arise and seek
For her maker meek:
And the desart wild.
Become a garden mild.

In the southern clime,
Where the summers prime,
Never fades away;
Lovely Lyca lay.

Seven summers old
Lovely Lyca told,
She had wanderd long,
Hearing wild birds song.

Sweet sleep come to me
Underneath this tree;
Do father, mother weep.—
Where can Lyca sleep.

Lost in desart wild
Is your little child.
How can Lyca sleep.
If her mother weep.

If her heart does ake,
Then let Lyca wake;
If my mother sleep,
Lyca shall not weep.

Frowning frowning night,
O'er this desart bright,
Let thy moon arise,
While I close my eyes.

Sleeping Lyca lay;
While the beasts of prey,
Come from caverns deep,
Viewd the maid asleep

The kingly lion stood
And the virgin viewd,
Then he gambold round
O'er the hallowd ground:

Leopards, tygers play,
Round her as she lay;
While the lion old,
Bow'd his mane of gold,

And her bosom lick,
And upon her neck,
From his eyes of flame,
Ruby tears there came;

While the lioness,
Loos'd her slender dress,
And naked they convey'd
To caves the sleeping maid.

The Little Girl Found

All the night in woe,
Lyca's parents go:
Over vallies deep.
While the desarts weep.

Tired and woe-begone.
Hoarse with making moan:
Arm in arm seven days.
They trac'd the desart ways.

Seven nights they sleep.
Among shadows deep:
And dream they see their child
Starv'd in desart wild.

Pale thro' pathless ways
The fancied image strays.

Famish'd

Leopards, tygers play,
Round her as she lay;
While the lion old,
Bow'd his mane of gold,

And her bosom lick,
And upon her neck,
From his eyes of flame,
Ruby tears there came;

While the lioness,
Loos'd her slender dress,
And naked they convey'd
To caves the sleeping maid.

The Little Girl Found

All the night in woe,
Lyca's parents go;
Over vallies deep,
While the desarts weep.

Tired and woe-begone,
Hoarse with making moan:
Arm in arm seven days,
They trac'd the desart ways.

Seven nights they sleep,
Among shadows deep:
And dream they see their child
Starv'd in desart wild.

Pale thro' pathless ways
The fancied image strays,

Famish'd, weeping, weak
With hollow piteous shriek

Rising from unrest,
The trembling woman prest,
With feet of weary woe;
She could no further go.

In his arms he bore.
Her arm'd with sorrow sore:
Till before their way,
A couching lion lay.

Turning back was vain,
Soon his heavy mane.
Bore them to the ground;
Then he stalk'd around.

Smelling to his prey,
But their fears allay.
When he licks their hands:
And silent by them stands.

They look upon his eyes
Fill'd with deep surprise:
And wondering behold.
A spirit arm'd in gold.

On his head a crown
On his shoulders down,
Flow'd his golden hair.
Gone was all their care.

Follow me he said,
Weep not for the maid;
In my palace deep.
Lyca lies asleep.

Then they followed,
Where the vision led;
And saw their sleeping child,
Among tygers wild.

To this day they dwell
In a lonely dell
Nor fear the wolvish howl,
Nor the lions growl.

Then sad weeping, weak
With hollow piteous shriek

Rising from unrest,
The trembling woman prest,
With feet of weary woe;
She could no further go.

In his arms he bore,
Her arm'd with sorrow sore;
Till before their way,
A couching lion lay.

Turning back was vain,
Soon his heavy mane,
Bore them to the ground;
Then he stalk'd around.

Smelling to his prey,
But their fears allay,
When he licks their hands;
And silent by them stands.

They look upon his eyes
Fill'd with deep surprise;
And wondering behold,
A spirit arm'd in gold.

On his head a crown,
On his shoulders down,
Flow'd his golden hair.
Gone was all their care.

Follow me he said,
Weep not for the maid;
In my palace deep,
Lyca lies asleep.

Then they followed,
Where the vision led;
And saw their sleeping child,
Among tygers wild.

To this day they dwell
In a lonely dell;
Nor fear the wolvish howl,
Nor the lions growl.

THE Chimney Sweeper

A little black thing among the snow:
Crying weep, weep, in notes of woe!
Where are thy father & mother? say?
They are both gone up to the church to pray.

Because I was happy upon the heath.
And smil'd among the winters snow:
They clothed me in the clothes of death.
And taught me to sing the notes of woe.

And because I am happy. & dance & sing.
They think they have done me no injury:
And are gone to praise God & his Priest & King
Who make up a heaven of our misery.

THE Chimney Sweeper

A little black thing among the snow:
Crying weep, weep, in notes of woe!
Where are thy father & mother? say?
They are both gone up to the church to pray.

Because I was happy upon the heath.
And smil'd among the winters snow:
They clothed me in the clothes of death.
And taught me to sing the notes of woe.

And because I am happy, & dance & sing,
They think they have done me no injury:
And are gone to praise God & his Priest & King
Who make up a heaven of our misery.

38

NURSES Song

When the voices of children. are heard on the green
And whisprings are in the dale:
The days of my youth rise fresh in my mind,
My face turns green and pale.

Then come home my children. the sun is gone down
And the dews of night arise
Your spring & your day. are wasted in play
And your winter and night in disguise.

NURSES Song

When the voices of children, are heard on the green
And whisprings are in the dale:
The days of my youth rise fresh in my mind,
My face turns green and pale.

Then come home my children, the sun is gone down
And the dews of night arise
Your spring & your day. are wasted in play
And your winter and night in disguise.

39

The SICK ROSE

O Rose thou art sick.
The invisible worm.
That flies in the night
In the howling storm:

Has found out thy bed
Of crimson joy:
And his dark secret love
Does thy life destroy.

THE FLY.

Little Fly
Thy summers play,
My thoughtless hand
Has brush'd away.

Am not I
A fly like thee?
Or art not thou
A man like me?

For I dance
And drink & sing;
Till some blind hand
Shall brush my wing.

If thought is life
And strength & breath;
And the want
Of thought is death;

Then am I
A happy fly,
If I live,
Or if I die.

The Angel

I Dreamt a Dream! what can it mean?
And that I was a maiden Queen:
Guarded by an Angel mild;
Witless woe, was neer beguil'd!

And I wept both night and day
And he wip'd my tears away
And I wept both day and night
And hid from him my hearts delight

So he took his wings and fled:
Then the morn blush'd rosy red:
I dried my tears & armd my fears,
With ten thousand shields and spears.

Soon my Angel came again;
I was arm'd, he came in vain:
For the time of youth was fled
And grey hairs were on my head

The Angel

I Dreamt a Dream! what can it mean?
And that I was a maiden Queen:
Guarded by an Angel mild;
Witless woe, was ne'er beguil'd!

And I wept both night and day
And he wip'd my tears away
And I wept both day and night
And hid from him my hearts delight

So he took his wings and fled;
Then the morn blush'd rosy red;
I dried my tears & arm'd my fears,
With ten thousand shields and spears.

Soon my Angel came again;
I was arm'd, he came in vain:
For the time of youth was fled
And grey hairs were on my head

42

The Tyger.

Tyger Tyger. burning bright,
In the forests of the night;
What immortal hand or eye.
Could frame thy fearful symmetry?

In what distant deeps or skies.
Burnt the fire of thine eyes?
On what wings dare he aspire?
What the hand, dare sieze the fire?

And what shoulder, & what art,
Could twist the sinews of thy heart?
And when thy heart began to beat.
What dread hand? & what dread feet?

What the hammer? what the chain,
In what furnace was thy brain?
What the anvil? what dread grasp.
Dare its deadly terrors clasp?

When the stars threw down their spears
And water'd heaven with their tears:
Did he smile his work to see?
Did he who made the Lamb make thee?

Tyger Tyger burning bright,
In the forests of the night:
What immortal hand or eye,
Dare frame thy fearful symmetry?

My Pretty ROSE TREE

A flower was offerd to me;
Such a flower as May never bore.
But I said I've a Pretty Rose-tree.
And I passed the sweet flower o'er.

Then I went to my Pretty Rose-tree:
To tend her by day and by night.
But my Rose turnd away with jealousy:
And her thorns were my only delight.

AH! SUN-FLOWER

Ah Sun-flower! weary of time.
Who countest the steps of the Sun:
Seeking after that sweet golden clime
Where the travellers journey is done.

Where the Youth pined away with desire,
And the pale Virgin shrouded in snow:
Arise from their graves and aspire.
Where my Sun-flower wishes to go.

THE LILLY

The modest Rose puts forth a thorn:
The humble Sheep. a threatning horn:
While the Lilly white, shall in Love delight,
Nor a thorn nor a threat stain her beauty bright

My Pretty ROSE TREE

A flower was offerd to me;
Such a flower as May never bore.
But I said I've a Pretty Rose-tree,
And I passed the sweet flower o'er.

Then I went to my Pretty Rose-tree:
To tend her by day and by night.
But my Rose turnd away with jealousy:
And her thorns were my only delight.

AH! SUN-FLOWER

Ah Sun-flower! weary of time,
Who countest the steps of the Sun:
Seeking after that sweet golden clime
Where the travellers journey is done.

Where the Youth pined away with desire,
And the pale Virgin shrouded in snow:
Arise from their graves and aspire,
Where my Sun-flower wishes to go.

THE LILLY

The modest Rose puts forth a thorn:
The humble Sheep, a threatning horn:
While the Lilly white, shall in Love delight,
Nor a thorn nor a threat stain her beauty bright

The GARDEN of LOVE

I went to the Garden of Love.
And saw what I never had seen:
A Chapel was built in the midst,
Where I used to play on the green.

And the gates of this Chapel were shut,
And Thou shalt not, writ over the door;
So I turn'd to the Garden of Love,
That so many sweet flowers bore,

And I saw it was filled with graves,
And tomb-stones where flowers should be:
And Priests in black gowns, were walking their rounds,
And binding with briars, my joys & desires.

The GARDEN of LOVE

I went to the Garden of Love.
And saw what I never had seen;
A Chapel was built in the midst,
Where I used to play on the green.

And the gates of this Chapel were shut,
And Thou shalt not, writ over the door;
So I turnd to the Garden of Love,
That so many sweet flowers bore.

And I saw it was filled with graves,
And tomb-stones where flowers should be:
And Priests in black gowns, were walking their
    rounds,
And binding with briars, my joys & desires

45

The Little Vagabond

Dear Mother, dear Mother, the Church is cold,
But the Ale-house is healthy & pleasant & warm:
Besides I can tell where I am use'd well,
Such usage in heaven will never do well.

But if at the Church they would give us some Ale.
And a pleasant fire, our souls to regale:
We'd sing and we'd pray all the live-long day:
Nor ever once wish from the Church to stray.

Then the Parson might preach & drink & sing.
And we'd be as happy as birds in the spring:
And modest dame Lurch, who is always at Church
Would not have bandy children nor fasting nor birch

And God like a father rejoicing to see.
His children as pleasant and happy as he:
Would have no more quarrel with the Devil or the Barrel
But kiss him & give him both drink and apparel.

The Little Vagabond

Dear Mother, dear Mother, the Church is cold,
But the Ale-house is healthy & pleasant & warm;
Besides I can tell where I am used well,
Such usage in heaven will never do well.

But if at the Church they would give us some Ale,
And a pleasant fire, our souls to regale;
We'd sing and we'd pray all the live-long day;
Nor ever once wish from the Church to stray.

Then the Parson might preach & drink & sing,
And we'd be as happy as birds in the spring;
And modest dame Lurch, who is always at Church,
Would not have bandy children nor fasting nor birch.

And God like a father rejoicing to see,
His children as pleasant and happy as he:
Would have no more quarrel with the Devil or the Barrel,
But kiss him & give him both drink and apparel.

LONDON

I wander thro' each charter'd street.
Near where the charter'd Thames does flow
And mark in every face I meet
Marks of weakness, marks of woe.

In every cry of every Man.
In every Infants cry of fear.
In every voice; in every ban.
The mind-forg'd manacles I hear

How the Chimney-sweepers cry
Every blackning Church appalls.
And the hapless Soldiers sigh
Runs in blood down Palace walls

But most thro' midnight streets I hear
How the youthful Harlots curse
Blasts the new-born Infants tear
And blights with plagues the Marriage hearse

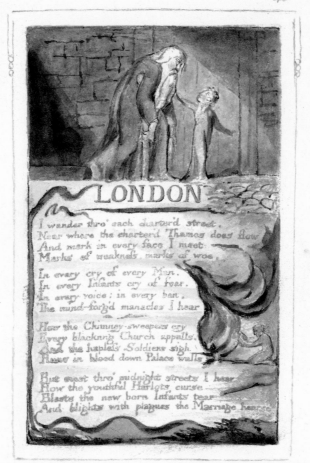

LONDON

I wander thro' each charter'd street,
Near where the charter'd Thames does flow
And mark in every face I meet
Marks of weakness, marks of woe.

In every cry of every Man,
In every Infants cry of fear,
In every voice: in every ban,
The mind-forg'd manacles I hear

How the Chimney-sweepers cry
Every blackning Church appalls,
And the hapless Soldiers sigh,
Runs in blood down Palace walls

But most thro' midnight streets I hear
How the youthful Harlots curse
Blasts the new born Infants tear
And blights with plagues the Marriage hearse

47

The Human Abstract.

Pity would be no more,
If we did not make somebody Poor;
And Mercy no more could be.
If all were as happy as we;

And mutual fear brings peace;
Till the selfish loves increase.
Then Cruelty knits a snare,
And spreads his baits with care.

He sits down with holy fears.
And waters the ground with tears:
Then Humility takes its root
Underneath his foot.

Soon spreads the dismal shade
Of Mystery over his head;
And the Catterpiller and Fly.
Feed on the Mystery.

And it bears the fruit of Deceit.
Ruddy and sweet to eat:
And the Raven his nest has made
In its thickest shade.

The Gods of the earth and sea,
Sought thro' Nature to find this Tree
But their search was all in vain:
There grows one in the Human Brain

The Human Abstract.

Pity would be no more,
If we did not make somebody Poor:
And Mercy no more could be,
If all were as happy as we;

And mutual fear brings peace;
Till the selfish loves increase.
Then Cruelty knits a snare,
And spreads his baits with care.

He sits down with holy fears,
And waters the ground with tears:
Then Humility takes its root
Underneath his foot.

Soon spreads the dismal shade
Of Mystery over his head;
And the Catterpiller and Fly,
Feed on the Mystery.

And it bears the fruit of Deceit,
Ruddy and sweet to eat;
And the Raven his nest has made
In its thickest shade.

The Gods of the earth and sea,
Sought thro' Nature to find this Tree
But their search was all in vain:
There grows one in the Human Brain

48

INFANT SORROW

My mother groand! my father wept,
Into the dangerous world I leapt:
Helpless, naked, piping loud:
Like a fiend hid in a cloud.

Struggling in my fathers hands:
Striving against my swadling bands:
Bound and weary I thought best
To sulk upon my mothers breast.

INFANT SORROW

My mother groand! my father wept.
Into the dangerous world I leapt:
Helpless, naked, piping loud:
Like a fiend hid in a cloud.

Struggling in my fathers hands:
Striving against my swadling bands:
Bound and weary I thought best
To sulk upon my mothers breast.

49

A POISON TREE.

I was angry with my friend;
I told my wrath, my wrath did end.
I was angry with my foe:
I told it not. my wrath did grow.

And I waterd it in fears,
Night & morning with my tears:
And I sunned it with smiles,
And with soft deceitful wiles.

And it grew both day and night,
Till it bore an apple bright.
And my foe beheld it shine,
And he knew that it was mine.

And into my garden stole.
When the night had veild the pole;
In the morning glad I see,
My foe outstretchd beneath the tree.

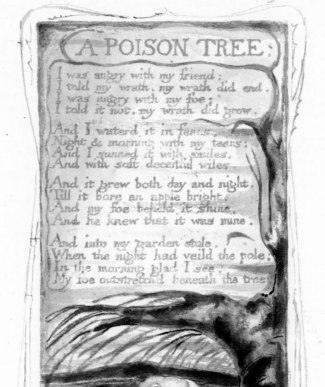

A Little BOY Lost

Nought loves another as itself
Nor venerates another so.
Nor is it possible to Thought
A greater than itself to know:

And Father. how can I love you,
Or any of my brothers more?
I love you like the little bird
That picks up crumbs around the door.

The Priest sat by and heard the child,
In trembling zeal he siez'd his hair:
He led him by his little coat:
And all admir'd the Priestly care.

And standing on the altar high.
Lo what a fiend is here! said he:
One who sets reason up for judge
Of our most holy Mystery.

The weeping child could not be heard,
The weeping parents wept in vain:
They strip'd him to his little shirt.
And bound him in an iron chain.

And burn'd him in a holy place.
Where many had been burn'd before:
The weeping parents wept in vain.
Are such things done on Albions shore.

A Little BOY Lost

Nought loves another as itself
Nor venerates another so,
Nor is it possible to Thought
A greater than itself to know:

And Father, how can I love you,
Or any of my brothers more?
I love you like the little bird
That picks up crumbs around the door.

The Priest sat by and heard the child,
In trembling zeal he siez'd his hair:
He led him by his little coat:
And all admir'd the Priestly care.

And standing on the altar high,
Lo what a fiend is here! said he:
One who sets reason up for judge
Of our most holy Mystery.

The weeping child could not be heard,
The weeping parents wept in vain:
They strip'd him to his little shirt,
And bound him in an iron chain.

And burn'd him in a holy place,
Where many had been burn'd before:
The weeping parents wept in vain.
Are such things done on Albions shore.

A Little GIRL Lost

Children of the future Age.
Reading this indignant page;
Know that in a former time.
Love! sweet Love! was thought a crime.

In the Age of Gold,
Free from winters cold:
Youth and maiden bright.
To the holy light,
Naked in the sunny beams delight.

Once a youthful pair
Fill'd with softest care;
Met in garden bright.
Where the holy light,
Had just removd the curtains of the night.

There in rising day.
On the grass they play:
Parents were afar;
Strangers came not near:
And the maiden soon forgot her fear.

Tired with kisses sweet
They agree to meet,
When the silent sleep
Waves o'er heavens deep:
And the weary tired wanderers weep.

To her father white
Came the maiden bright:
But his loving look,
Like the holy book,
All her tender limbs with terror shook

Ona! pale and weak!
To thy father speak:
O the trembling fear!
O the dismal care!
That shakes the blossoms of my hoary hair

A Little GIRL Lost

Children of the future Age,
Reading this indignant page;
Know that in a former time,
Love! sweet Love! was thought a crime.

In the Age of Gold,
Free from winters cold;
Youth and maiden bright,
To the holy light,
Naked in the sunny beams delight.

Once a youthful pair
Fill'd with softest care;
Met in garden bright,
Where the holy light,
Had just removd the curtains of the night.

There in rising day,
On the grass they play:
Parents were afar:
Strangers came not near:
And the maiden soon forgot her fear.

Tired with kisses sweet
They agree to meet,
When the silent sleep
Waves o'er heavens deep;
And the weary tired wanderers weep.

To her father white
Came the maiden bright:
But his loving look,
Like the holy book,
All her tender limbs with terror shook.

Ona! pale and weak!
To thy father speak:
O the trembling fear!
O the dismal care!
That shakes the blossoms of my hoary hair

52

To Tirzah

Whate'er is Born of Mortal Birth,
Must be consumed with the Earth
To rise from Generation free:
Then what have I to do with thee?

The Sexes sprung from Shame & Pride
Blowd in the morn; in evening died
But Mercy changd Death into Sleep;
The Sexes rose to work & weep.

Thou Mother of my Mortal part.
With cruelty didst mould my Heart.
And with false self-decieving tears.
Didst bind my Nostrils Eyes & Ears

Didst close my Tongue in senseless clay
And me to Mortal Life betray:
The Death of Jesus set me free.
Then what have I to do with thee?

It is Raised
a Spiritual Body

To Tirzah

Whate'er is Born of Mortal Birth,
Must be consumed with the Earth
To rise from Generation free;
Then what have I to do with thee?

The Sexes sprung from Shame & Pride
Blow'd in the morn; in evening died
But Mercy changd Death into Sleep;
The Sexes rose to work & weep.

Thou Mother of my Mortal part.
With cruelty didst mould my Heart.
And with false self-deceiving tears,
Didst bind my Nostrils Eyes & Ears.

Didst close my Tongue in senseless clay
And me to Mortal Life betray:
The Death of Jesus set me free,
Then what have I to do with thee?

It is Raised a Spiritual Body

The School Boy

I love to rise in a summer morn,
When the birds sing on every tree;
The distant huntsman winds his horn,
And the sky-lark sings with me.
O! what sweet company.

But to go to school in a summer morn,
O! it drives all joy away;
Under a cruel eye outworn.
The little ones spend the day,
In sighing and dismay.

Ah! then at times I drooping sit,
And spend many an anxious hour,
Nor in my book can I take delight,
Nor sit in learnings bower,
Worn thro' with the dreary shower.

How can the bird that is born for joy,
Sit in a cage and sing.
How can a child when fears annoy.
But droop his tender wing.
And forget his youthful spring.

O! father & mother. if buds are nip'd,
And blossoms blown away,
And if the tender plants are strip'd
Of their joy in the springing day,
By sorrow and cares dismay.

How shall the summer arise in joy.
Or the summer fruits appear.
Or how shall we gather what griefs destroy
Or bless the mellowing year.
When the blasts of winter appear.

The School Boy

I love to rise in a summer morn,
When the birds sing on every tree;
The distant huntsman winds his horn,
And the sky-lark sings with me.
O! what sweet company.

But to go to school in a summer morn,
O! it drives all joy away;
Under a cruel eye outworn,
The little ones spend the day,
In sighing and dismay.

Ah! then at times I drooping sit,
And spend many an anxious hour,
Nor in my book can I take delight,
Nor sit in learnings bower,
Worn thro' with the dreary shower.

How can the bird that is born for joy,
Sit in a cage and sing,
How can a child when fears annoy,
But droop his tender wing,
And forget his youthful spring.

O! father & mother, if buds are nip'd,
And blossoms blown away,
And if the tender plants are striped
Of their joy in the springing day,
By sorrow and cares dismay.

How shall the summer rise in joy,
Or the summer fruits appear,
Or how shall we gather what griefs destroy
Or bless the mellowing year,
When the blasts of winter appear.

54

The Voice of the Ancient Bard.

Youth of delight come hither.
And see the opening morn,
Image of truth new born.
Doubt is fled & clouds of reason.
Dark disputes & artful teazing,
Folly is an endless maze,
Tangled roots perplex her ways,
How many have fallen there!
They stumble all night over bones of the dead:
And feel they know not what but care;
And wish to lead others when they should be led

The Voice of the
Ancient Bard.

Youth of delight come hither.
And see the opening morn,
Image of truth new born.
Doubt is fled & clouds of reason,
Dark disputes & artful teazing.
Folly is an endless maze,
Tangled roots perplex her ways,
How many have fallen there!
They stumble all night over bones of the dead;
And feel they know not what but care;
And wish to lead others when they should be led.

PLATES FROM OTHER COPIES
Figs. 1–12

(references are to combined copies of *Songs of Innocence and of Experience*)

1 From 'The Ecchoing Green' (copy B, *British Museum Print Room*)
2 From 'A Cradle Song' (copy B)
3 'Infant Sorrow' (copy A, *British Museum Print Room*)
4 Plate a (copy B)
5 Plate b (posthumous impression, *Keynes Bequest, Fitzwilliam Museum, Cambridge*)
6 Experience Frontispiece (copy T, *British Museum Print Room*)
7 'The Tyger' (copy T)
8 'The Divine Image' (copy B)
9 'The Divine Image' (copy R, *Fitzwilliam Museum, Cambridge*)
10 'The Divine Image' (copy AA, *Fitzwilliam Museum, Cambridge*)
11 From 'The Little Black Boy' (copy B)
12 'The Little Boy lost' (copy B)

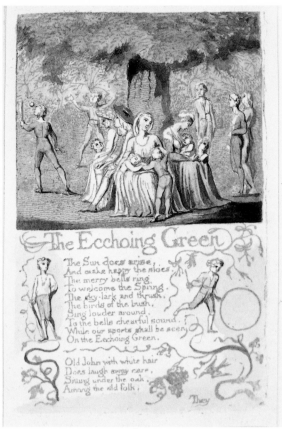

Fig. 1

Fig. 2

Fig. 3

Fig. 4

Fig. 5

Fig. 6

Fig. 7

Fig. 8

Fig. 9

Fig. 10

For when our souls have learn'd the heat to bear
The cloud will vanish we shall hear his voice.
Saying: come out from the grove my love & care.
And round my golden tent like lambs rejoice.

Thus did my mother say and kissed me.
And thus I say to little English boy.
When I from black and he from white cloud free.
And round the tent of God like lambs we joy:

I'll shade him from the heat till he can bear.
To lean in joy upon our fathers knee.
And then I'll stand and stroke his silver hair.
And be like him and he will then love me.

The Little Boy lost

Father, father where are you going
O do not walk so fast.
Speak father, speak to your little boy
Or else I shall be lost,

The night was dark no father was there
The child was wet with dew.
The mire was deep, & the child did weep
And away the vapour flew.

Fig. 11   Fig. 12

Commentary
on the text and the plates

Plate 1: Combined Title-page

SONGS

Of

INNOCENCE

and Of

EXPERIENCE

*Shewing the Two Contrary States
of the Human Soul*

The volume begins at the threshold of the fallen world. Adam and Eve, having covered their nakedness with fig leaves, depart from Eden. They are driven westward, towards a recognition of death. The flames that sweep over them correspond to the 'flaming sword' of the cherubim set to guard the tree of life (Genesis 3.23–24). But in Blake's work, flames often symbolise the power of imagination to consume the corrupt, finite world of the closed senses, and to open the individual to eternal life. In the light of this symbolism, the loss of paradise can be seen as a withdrawal rather than an expulsion: humanity lapses from a strenuously imaginative vision into a passive and limited view of its existence.[1] Adam bends over Eve as if to protect her from the heat, clutching his head in both hands, face hidden. His body is partly surrounded by gold flames. She looks upward and ahead, her mouth slightly open as if in wondering dread. From beneath her fingertips a scroll-like flame of red, purple, blue and gold runs across the foot of the page; a line of gold shines beneath her. In the upper part of the plate clouds lighten to rose, white and yellow, or darken to brown and black. Among them a 'bird of paradise' flies upward – a motif that recurs in the Innocence plates.[2] Its ascent contrasts with the human figures who incline to earth, and offers a reminder of the freedom they have lost. The design creates an effect of turbulent symmetry, in which glowing colours and extremes of light and shade are carefully balanced.[3] The lettering of the main title (except 'and') has has been heightened with gold. Scrolls rise or stream down from some of the letters. Barely discernable on the lower end of the first 'S', beside a rising green scroll, a tiny human figure stands. Another (shaded with gold) sits in front, bending forward, arms apparently outstretched.

The elaborate border with its coiling vines, scroll and leaves, offers intimations of hope that contrast with the catastrophe of the main design. The trellis which forms a gothic arch either side of the figures may remind us of the tradition of prophetic art that strives to keep the divine vision

---

[1] In *Europe* the fall is described as a withdrawal:

> Thought chang'd the infinite to a serpent; that which pitieth:
> To a devouring flame; and man fled from its face and hid
> In forests of night

$$(E\ 63;\ K\ 241)$$

On plate 14 of the *The Marriage of Heaven and Hell*, the Devil commands the cherub with the flaming sword to leave his guard at the tree of life 'and when he does, the whole creation will be consumed and appear infinite. and holy' (*E* 39, *K* 154).

[2] For convenience I have adopted Erdman's term for this motif (see *IB* 42).

[3] Bass notes that diagonal movement (like that from lower right to upper left here) is a recurring feature in the designs of the *Songs*: Eben Bass, '*Songs of Innocence and of Experience:* The Thrust of Design', *Visionary Forms Dramatic* edited by David V. Erdman and John E. Grant (Princeton, 1970), pp. 196–213.

alive in the fallen world. A comparable trellis border appears in Blake's Job series (plate 2), where it offers hope as Job falls.[4] Tiny pink flames appear either side, level with 'Innocence', perhaps indicating the inspirational potential of this state of the soul; three more, yellow and pink, appear at the top centre. The vine is traditionally an emblem of Christ (John 15.1, 5); here it may allude to the comforting presence of divinity in the fallen world. At the foot of the plate a grey briar, associated elsewhere in the *Songs* with repression and death (see plate 44), is surrounded by consuming fire.

[4] See David Bindman, *The Complete Graphic Works of William Blake* (London, 1978), no. 627.

Plate 2: Frontispiece to Songs of Innocence

This shady woodland scene offers a striking contrast to the fire and smoke of the previous plate. The foliage and the blue-violet of the piper's costume create an impression of coolness.[1] The image of the piper as shepherd announces the predominantly pastoral mode of *Innocence*, and illuminates the 'Introduction' on the following plate. There the piper becomes aware of his artistic vocation, and begins to direct his work towards an audience; the child symbolises the exuberant vision that inspires his songs. Here the piper is shown as if arrested in mid-stride, his pipe lowered. He looks up to the naked child who floats with outstretched arms upon a luminous cloud. Gold shines faintly around the child's head, and lightens the cloud's left edges. Behind the piper sheep graze peacefully, their fleece shaded abundantly with gold. The entwined trees on the right may be seen as emblems of love and harmony (see *E* 413, *K* 7); their gently curving lines are typical of Innocence. But if the enclosed woodland setting evokes security and a simple contentment, the piper is placed at a threshold – stepping through the frame made by the trees.[2] The contrast between the sheep looking down to graze and his upward glance emphasizes his coming to consciousness. He doesn't share the child's smile.

There are gold highlights on the twined trunks, in the vegetation above the cloud, between the piper's feet, on his pipe and, more faintly, on his costume. The border is composed of very fine orange and green trellises supporting vines that break into coils opposite the child. There are vague suggestions of roots along the bottom of the plate.

[1] Costumes that reveal the human form like this appear elsewhere in Innocence (Coleridge wondered whether Blake depicted garments 'or the body incised and scored out': *BR*, 252). Leader relates this clothing to the skeleton suits of the 1780s, inspired by Rousseau and his followers, 'designed to facilitate free and easy movements in the young, and to distinguish them, clearly, from their parents' (*Reading Blake's Songs*, p. 68).

[2] The piper steps forward with his left foot here. In the Experience frontispiece his right foot is forward. Wicksteed suggests that a 'Right and Left symbolism' is used here, right associated with spiritual values, left with material: Joseph H. Wicksteed, *Blake's Innocence and Experience* (London, 1928), p. 37.

Plate 3: Title-page for Songs of Innocence

SONGS
of
Innocence
1789
The Author & Printer W Blake

The colouring in the scene below the title suggests twilight. In the foreground a young woman in a white cap – a nurse or mother – sits on a stout chair with a boy and girl at her knee. The children study a book which she holds open on her lap (the girl appears to be turning a page). The vine-encircled tree to the right extends its leaves over the children and displays above the word 'Innocence' five orange fruits. Contemporary children's books often included prints of adults teaching children (see Introduction). Here the presence of the fruit tree relates the children at their book to the myth of Eden. In this context the fall is evoked as an event that is re-enacted in the life of each individual: the innocent child must taste the fruit of the tree of knowledge (as yet seemingly out of reach) and enter the state of Experience. The fragility of Innocence is suggested at the outset. In the *Songs* the adult's role as guardian is frequently presented in ambiguous terms: the guardian protects the child, but the child is therefore at the mercy of its protector. The process of education may be joyful or destructive (see plate 53). The nurse's stiff posture and enigmatic expression may point to the central ambiguity, although the boy has a hint of a smile.

Despite the sombre tones here, the impression created by the plate as a whole is far from bleak. The extraordinary colouring of the upper sky (blue, yellow and rose, darkening to grey, purple and black) contrasts with the scene below, while the blue and gold letters of the title are vigorously animated. Flame-like vegetation bursts upwards or flows downwards from 'SONGS'. Within the letters tiny figures appear: one can be seen indistinctly behind the first 'S'; an open-armed child kneels in the 'O'; a minute being stands above the first upright of the 'N' and a winged angel leans against the downstroke to write in a book; a robed figure holds the top of the 'G' with raised arms; another figure sits in the lower curve of the last 'S'. Against the 'I' of 'Innocence' leans a piper wearing a wide-brimmed hat. Three birds soar around the letters (one above the 'N' of 'SONGS', another below the first 'S', a third to the right of the piper). The various activities and the general impression of movement here suggest, perhaps, the visionary world that may be opened, or closed, by the activity of reading.

There is gold in the flame-like forms at the top of the page, on the winged angel, the piper's hat and at the end of his pipe, down the left side of the tree trunk, at the hem of the nurse's skirt, and in a frame around the panel which identifies the author at the foot of the page. To the right of the tree the date '1789' appears. The border is a simple symmetrical pattern of curving scrolls suggesting flames or leaves.

Plate 4: Introduction

Piping down the valleys wild
Piping songs of pleasant glee
On a cloud I saw a child.
And he laughing said to me.

Pipe a song about a Lamb:
So I piped with merry chear,
Piper pipe that song again—
So I piped, he wept to hear.

Drop thy pipe thy happy pipe
Sing thy songs of happy chear,
So I sung the same again
While he wept with joy to hear

Piper sit thee down and write
In a book that all may read—
So he vanish'd from my sight
And I pluck'd a hollow reed

And I made a rural pen,
And I stain'd the water clear,
And I wrote my happy songs,
Every child may joy to hear.

The entwined and looping trees of yellowy green that stand at either side of the text recall the Tree of Jesse as depicted in church windows and medieval manuscripts.[1] The minute vignettes inside the loops are mostly indistinct (although partially reinforced in ink). Taking the panels from top to bottom, on the left are: 1. a seated adult with a standing child (recalling plate 3); 2. a naked figure bursting through the loop with arms outstretched (the posture similar to that shown in 'Albion Rose' or 'Glad Day');[2] 3. a figure leaning forwards, arms reaching down to (perhaps) a grazing sheep; 4. a half-drawn figure looking upward, with foliage above and to the left. On the right are: 1. a bird flying upward; 2. a figure sitting cross-legged, resting head on hand (perhaps related to the figure of Jesse in the Sistine ceiling fresco);[3] 3. a standing figure who reaches out as if to feed two birds flying nearby; 4. two figures side by side as if conferring. Tiny vines coil about the trees, some pushing into the spaces between stanzas, some hanging tiny leaves above the title. The design creates the impression of a carefully ordered variety – like the sequence of songs that will follow. The title and its underlining are gold.

The Tree of Jesse motif emphasizes the Christian context of the work, and points to the spiritual significance of the accompanying lyric, in which the piper sings 'a song about a Lamb'. The absence of quotation marks is a significant feature of several of the songs.[4] Here it may encourage us to see the child as an aspect of the piper's own creativity. The poem seems uncomplicated: the rhythms, repetitions and diction create an effect of child-like simplicity. But although the poem seems a 'happy' song, it is not unambiguous. The laughing child who captures the piper's attention inspires a sense of mission and of consequences. As the piper is transformed into a scribe, hints of unease appear (the disappearance of the child, the 'hollow' reed and 'stain'd' water) which point to the difference between the carefree inspiration of the moment, and the careful labour of the artist whose works 'may' please his intended audience.[5]

A line of gold crosses the plate beneath the text, forming the bank of a river. The lower edge of the plate forms the nearside bank of brown and gold. Several other Innocence plates (7, 8, 10, 12, 23, 24) have a similar motif. As the river forms a visual boundary, flowing between the reader and the text, it may suggest the mental transition the experienced reader must make in order to enter into the spirit of the Innocence poems (a kind of baptism).

The border has several elements: curving scroll-like forms of vegetation issue from the top

[1] Anthony Blunt, *The Art of William Blake* (Columbia, 1959), p. 48.

[2] Martin Butlin, *The Paintings and Drawings of William Blake*, 2 vols. (New Haven and London, 1981), II, 331–2.

[3] Robert Essick's suggestion about the Sistine fresco is recorded by David Erdman, *IB* 45. As Erdmans's descriptions show, the details in the vignettes vary in other copies.

[4] See David W. Lindsay, *Blake: Songs of Innocence and Experience* (London, 1989), p. 19.

[5] Glen notes that the poem describes 'an energy that is, at first, expressive rather than communicative: but as the poem proceeds it becomes channelled and delimited': Heather Glen, *Vision and Disenchantment* (Cambridge, 1983), p. 65.

Plate 5: The Shepherd

How sweet is the Shepherds sweet lot,
From the morn to the evening he strays:
He shall follow his sheep all the day
And his tongue shall be filled with praise.

For he hears the lambs innocent call.
And he hears the ewes tender reply,
He is watchful while they are in peace,
For they know when their Shepherd is nigh.

corners, while the straight lines down either side suggest stems (or folds of drapery, or even the pages of an open book). At the bottom gold lines reinforced with black suggest roots.

A glow of yellow behind the dark blue and purple of the distant hill indicates sunrise or sunset. The scene, with its deep green foliage and large flock, is an image of peaceful abundance. In the richly-coloured sky, to the left, a bird of paradise flies up displaying wings of blue streaked with violet; three or four smaller birds appear close by. The shepherd's blue costume recalls that of the piper-shepherd in plate 2 (although the style is different). This shepherd, crook in hand and with a scrip at his side, is closer to his sheep, one of whom returns his gaze. To the right a thick vine twines around the dark brown trunk of the tree, sending out four bells. Gold is used liberally here – in the title (including the vines curling from the first word), in the shepherd's hair, in faint highlights on the foreground tree (both trunk and foliage) and on the vine, and in the fleece of the sheep.

The poem evokes and transforms the biblical image of the good shepherd. Throughout the Bible the sheep that has gone astray denotes backsliding or disobedience, while the shepherd's care for his flock represents spiritual guidance.[1] The New Testament may give more emphasis to the self-sacrificing nature of the shepherd, but it also insists on his guiding role ('they shall hear my voice', John 10.16). Here the shepherd strays, follows and hears his flock. He protects without controlling, and so embodies a love that is unconditional. The posture of the shepherd in the design, at once attentive and relaxed, helps to emphasize this.

Despite the affirmative tone of the poem, there is a sense here of the limitations of a life given to straying from the 'morn to the evening'. The repetition of 'sweet' in the first line is potentially cloying, and casts a shadow of irony over the notion that the Shepherd's tongue shall be 'filled' with praise. The contentment here seems fragile, a suggestion reinforced by the border – a protective arbour of slender green stems or trees either side with, across the top, delicate grey-brown branches and stippled green leaves. Dark roots appear at the bottom.

---

[1] For the image of stray sheep see, for example, Psalm 119.176; Isaiah 53.6; Matthew 18.12; for the shepherd as spiritual guide see Psalms 23.3; 80.1; Isaiah 40.11; Ezekiel 34.13. Blake's poem may be compared with Charles Wesley's 'Jesu, Shepherd of the sheep', which develops the traditional distinction between the guiding shepherd and the soul 'never at one stay': *A Collection of Hymns*, edited by John Wesley (London, 1781), p. 178.

Plates 6–7: The Ecchoing Green

The Sun does arise,
And make happy the skies.
The merry bells ring,
To welcome the Spring.
The sky-lark and thrush,
The birds of the bush,
Sing louder around,
To the bells chearful sound.
While our sports shall be seen
On the Ecchoing Green.

Old John with white hair
Does laugh away care,
Sitting under the oak,
Among the old folk.

They laugh at our play,
And soon they all say,
Such such were the joys.
When we all girls & boys.
In our youth time were seen,
On the Ecchoing Green.

Till the little ones weary
No more can be merry
The sun does descend,
And our sports have an end:
Round the laps of their mothers.
Many sisters and brothers,
Like birds in their nest.
Are ready for rest;
And sport no more seen,
On the darkening Green.

With its lilting rhythms, chiming couplets and refrain, this song is full of echoes. It is not only space which echoes: the shifts in tenses create an echoing through time. The poem spans the rising and setting of the sun, which frames an internal pattern of expectations and memories. In the first stanza the sun and the bells (both measures of time) stimulate an expanding mood of joy and harmony, while the shift to the future tense in the last couplet extends the movement outwards to a potential audience. The second stanza puts us more clearly in a temporal world of age and care, but here the feeling of joyful communion evokes memories of a past echoed in the present. Sport has become recreation in the fullest sense, as the older generation sees its own joy enacted in the younger.[1] The third stanza, in which the weary children 'No more can be merry', emphasizes the natural limits to joy. The speaker, apparently younger than the old folk and the mothers, but older than 'the little ones', reveals a dawning awareness of the passage of time, off-set by a sense of continuity and of the potential for happiness. The recognition that in time 'our sports have an end' has both a present and future significance, as well as echoing the past.

In the first plate, the symmetrical composition of the upper design holds the different generations together as a unified group, reinforcing the suggestions of social harmony in the poem. The figures beneath the dense green canopy of the oak are drawn finely. There are more spectators than players here: like the poem, the design emphasizes that the sports 'are seen'. At the left two boys play at bat and ball on the green, while at the right three youths stand as if watching them. Behind the players are bushes or a hedge, beyond which rise the branches of trees suggested by delicate black and green strokes at the left of the tree, and fine brown outlines to the right. Against the glow of the sky the branches create a dynamic, luminous mottling. Sitting around the base of the oak are three generations. At the left, the white-haired man in a green suit and blue wide-brimmed hat, who sits with hands on knees, corresponds to 'Old John'. With him are three nurses or mothers with 'little ones weary' at the knee and (at right) on the lap.

If the upper design encompasses both infancy and old age, the vines around the text in the lower portion of the plate display a comparable cycle of growth. One to the left, which curls up past a boy with a cricket bat, has leaves only. The blossoming vine that sprouts from the golden title has, as Erdman notes, 'very active sexual parts' (*IB* 47). A third, below the boy who bowls a golden hoop, bears grapes coloured green and purple (as if ripening), towards which a bird flies.

The lower half of the border is, at the bottom, a delicate green stripe, which turns brown at each side. The upper half sports flame-like leaves and, at the corners, spiralling vines.

[146]

On the second plate, a low angle of vision sets the figures against open sky. The warm colouring indicates sunset; a few fine stripes of gold and grey across the lower middle sky form cirrus clouds. After the sports, the players and watchers go home. As 'Old John' points the way for the children, his central position corresponds to that of the protective oak in the first plate. At the right sturdy twin grapevines curve up and part to form a partial frame for the text. Some critics associate the picking of the grapes here with the dawn of sexual awareness at adolescence, and see irony in the fact that the boy picking grapes at top left, and the one handing grapes to the young girl at the right, are out of sight of the adults.[2] But there seems to be no secrecy concerning the grapes: in this copy even an infant (in blue) carries some.[3] If the first plate illustrates the cycle of growth, this one shows a harvesting. Something is taken away from the scene, to be enjoyed in the future, like memories of past joy.

The composition makes use of simple colour contrasts and harmonies. The costumes differ somewhat from those in the first plate ('Old John's' hat, for example, is now sepia and black), no doubt because Blake is more concerned with the formal qualities of each design than with pictorial consistency. There are some fine details, such as the red spotted head scarf of the woman with a baby in her arms. The balancing of the white kite at the left with the white dress at the right seems typical of the concern with pattern. Three of the boys here appear to be in uniform (of yellow breeches and blue jacket or shirt). The pale blue, yellow and red of the costumes harmonise easily with each other, and with the sky, while the green of the old man's costume stands out, emphizing his central position. At the foot of the plate a river runs between green banks (the nearside bank barely visible). The border has delicate, serpentine green vine stems, with leaves and curling tendrils.

[1] In Michael Tolley's words, the sports as seen 'as echoed, as having been seen . . . so that we have a pleasant receding image of old folk . . . remembering the time when they too were young, and so on'. 'Blake's Songs of Spring', *William Blake: Essays in Honour of Sir Geoffrey Keynes*, edited by Morton D. Paley and Michael Phillips (Oxford, 1973), p. 107.

[2] See the discussion in Leader, *Reading Blake's Songs* (p. 86). As Lindsay notes (1989, p. 64), the poem recalls Goldsmith's description of village 'sports beneath the spreading tree', in *The Deserted Village* (lines 15–34). But there youthful sexuality and 'secret laughter' are a part of the sport, in which one can see 'The bashful virgin's sidelong looks of love / The matron's glance that would those looks reprove'.

[3] The infant's grapes are also visible in copy X of the *Songs*. In other copies they are not visible. See *IB* 47.

Plate 8: The Lamb

Little Lamb who made thee	Little Lamb I'll tell thee,
Dost thou know who made thee	Little Lamb Ill tell thee;
Gave thee life & bid thee feed.	He is called by thy name,
By the stream & o'er the mead;	For he calls himself a Lamb:
Gave thee clothing of delight.	He is meek & he is mild,
Softest clothing wooly bright;	He became a little child:
Gave thee such a tender voice.	I a child & thou a lamb,
Making all the vales rejoice:	We are called by his name,
Little Lamb who made thee	Little Lamb God bless thee,
Dost thou know who made thee	Little Lamb God bless thee.

In its theme, diction and tone this song resembles Charles Wesley's hymn 'Gentle Jesus meek and mild', as several critics have noted.[1] But the child-like perspective in Blake's poem excludes adult moralising of the kind found in Wesley.[2] The child may be repeating a lesson taught by an adult, but his understanding of the maker is expressed in his own delight in the Lamb. Divine love is associated with giving, protective care and rejoicing, but there is no mention of obedience or self-denial. If the initial question implies a distinction between maker and creature, the distinction is undermined in the second stanza by the child's sense of identity with both Lamb and 'little child'. In this vision, the child makes the incarnation a present reality for himself and in himself: his blessing of the Lamb is God's blessing.

The design provides a visual equivalent of the song's child-like vision of divine protection. Two slender, vine-encircled trees curve up to form a high arch, framing the scene. Over the text their entwined branches 'weave a shade' (see plates 16 and 26). The pastoral scene below the text is sunny and peaceful. It has links with others earlier in the sequence: the naked child who holds out his hands for a lamb to lick stands in the place of the shepherd of plate 5; the spreading oak recalls the tree on plate 6. On the thatch of the open-doored cottage two (indistinct) white birds are perched. Several elements in the scene modify the prevailing sense of security. The sky appears vaguely threatening in its darker shades: the area of bluish purple behind the cottage could be gathering cloud. The arching trees look fragile, and the protection they offer seems insubstantial. But the sky inside the arch shines with gold around the first stanza. More gold appears on the fleeces, on the thatch, in the title and the curling branches at its right. At the foot of the plate a river runs between green banks. The border is a simple rectangular frame of yellow and green, which carries a leafless vine with coiling tendrils.

[1] See, for example, Martha Winburn England and John Sparrow, *Hymns Unbidden: Donne, Herbert, Blake, Emily Dickinson and the Hymnographers* (New York, 1966), p. 44; Heather Glen, *Vision and Disenchantment*, p. 23.

[2] Nick Shrimpton notes, 'In most children's hymns animals simply perform ethical object lessons. Blake's animals do not come from this moral circus ring'. 'William Blake: Hell's Hymnbook', *Literature of the Romantic Period 1750–1850*, edited by R. T. Davies and B. G. Beatty (Liverpool, 1976), p. 25.

Plates 9–10: The Little Black Boy

My mother bore me in the southern wild,
And I am black, but O! my soul is white.
White as an angel is the English child:
But I am black as if bereav'd of light.

My mother taught me underneath a tree
And sitting down before the heat of day.
She took me on her lap and kissed me,
And pointing to the east began to say.

Look on the rising sun: there God does live
And gives his light. and gives his heat away.
And flowers and trees and beasts and men recieve
Comfort in morning joy in the noon day.

And we are put on earth a little space..
That we may learn to bear the beams of love.
And these black bodies and this sun-burnt face
Is but a cloud, and like a shady grove.

For when our souls have learn'd the heat to bear
The cloud will vanish we shall hear his voice.
Saying: come out from the grove my love & care.
And round my golden tent like lambs rejoice.

Thus did my mother say and kissed me.
And thus I say to little English boy.
When I from black and he from white cloud free,
And round the tent of God like lambs we joy:

Ill shade him from the heat till he can bear,
To lean in joy upon our fathers knee.
And then I'll stand and stroke his silver hair,
And be like him and he will then love me.

The song is apparently a response to the contemporary slave trade and, as Nurmi says, to 'the social and religious attitudes that made slavery possible'.[1] Blake characteristically approaches the subject from the point of view of a child victim (who is presumably in exile, recalling his homeland). In the first stanza the black boy sees his own condition in terms of traditional Christian thinking about colour and spiritual purity. But the rest of the song is concerned with the primitive faith he learned from his mother. The poem subverts the conventional view that those who lack the benefits of a Christian upbringing must dwell in spiritual darkness, a view expressed in Watts's hymn 'Praise for Birth and Education in a Christian Land':

> How do I pity those that dwell
> Where Ignorance and Darkness reigns;
> They know no Heav'n, they fear no Hell,
> Those endless Joys, those endless Pains.[2]

The little black boy fears no hell, not because he is ignorant, but because his vision of heaven involves an understanding of love and forgiveness that leaves no room for retribution.[3] As the first plate shows, this 'southern' faith is directly related to the experience of sun and shade in daily life. In the design at the top the rising sun, still touching the horizon, already has a spectacular appearance: its crimson-purple aurora is ringed by orange clouds and rays of gold.[4] Two red rays (and many faint gold ones) cross the distant green plain. The impression of fierce heat emphasizes the need for shade – which determines the black boy's thinking about God and about the body. He and his half-naked mother are the same dark brown colour as the tree that shades them. The dense foliage, rougher or wilder than its pastoral counterparts in plates 6 and 8, meets two thin branches from the tree at right, forming an arch over the sun. In the mother's vision, divine generosity is naturally associated with a heat that must be born. Her faith involves an implicit recognition that joy and pain may both be aspects of love.[5]

In the left margin, a delicate sapling bears a vine, which coils below the text and up into the right margin. At top right of stanza 2 a bird flies upwards. The title is gold, and there is gold beneath the last three lines of stanza 3, beneath stanza 4, and on the sapling at bottom left. In the bottom half of the border a grey, spiky outline suggests the trunk of a palm, at the top of which two round fruits are sketched. Above, three palm fronds hang down either side.

To a white boy whose conception of love has been limited by his 'Education in a Christian Land', the black boy's vision of heaven may well seem like a fiery hell at first. But this vision – in which there is mercy and forgiveness but no punishment – is essentially Christian, or so the designs imply. The tree that offers shade in the first plate is circled by a vine, while the second plate shows God as Jesus, the good shepherd. The temperate pastoral landscape offers a striking contrast to the tropical scene. The shepherd sits on a grassy bank beneath an arching willow tree. The light hues of his robe and the water near his feet add to the general impression of coolness. His white halo with golden rays is a counterpart to the burning sun of the previous plate. There is gold on the bank beneath his feet and body, and beneath the foliage of the willow above his head. More gold appears on the fleeces of the sheep, and in the left margin above the willow. At the shepherd's knee neither black nor white boy has lost his body. The freeing of the soul is seen primarily as a clarification of vision, a liberation from temporal prejudice.[6] Reversing the cultural assumptions of Christians like Watts, here the black boy introduces the white boy to Jesus.

In the right-hand margin two lily-like plants climb up by the text, from behind the willow tree below, perhaps emblems of love (see plate 43). A sinuous vine winds along the top and left of the text. In some copies there is another lily in the bottom left corner of the plate (*IB* 51). In this copy it is painted out. Traces of gold at top left partly cover the first three lines of text. More gold appears to the right of stanza 6, and below the final words of the last stanza. In the border, green rushes appear at either side, drawing level with the bottom of the text. The serpentine vine on the upper left side echoes the line of the vine inside the design, and is mirrored on the right.

[1] Martin K. Nurmi, *William Blake* (Kent State, 1976), p. 59. After the founding in 1787 of the Society

[149]

for the Abolition of the Slave Trade, a number of poets turned their attention to contemporary attitudes to Africans, and to the evils of slavery. In 1788 Cowper's 'The Morning Dream', Hugh Mulligans' *Poems Chiefly on Slavery and Oppression* and Samuel Jackson Pratt's *Humanity, or the Rights of Nature* appeared.

2 Isaac Watts, *Divine Songs*, edited by J. H. P. Padford (Oxford, 1971), p. 156.

3 Morton D. Paley suggests that Blake's view of the Black Boy's faith may have been influenced by Swedenborg's teaching 'that the inhabitants of Africa had preserved a direct intuition of God.' 'A New Heaven Is Begun: Blake and Swedenborgianism', *Blake: An Illustrated Quarterly* 12, no 2 (1979), pp. 64–90. See also the discussion of the Swedenborgian context by Kathleen Raine, *Blake and Tradition*, 2 vols (London, 1969), I, 10–15.

4 The mother's association of God with the rising sun echoes Isaiah 45.6; 59.19.

5 See *The Book of Urizen*, where the fall is associated with Urizen's attempt to separate joy from pain: 'I have sought for a joy without pain' (*E* 71, *K* 224). Blake's view of the black boy may also have been influenced by the sufferings of Job 30.30.

6 This conclusion is perhaps anticipated in the image of the body as a 'shady grove', which in this context connects prejudice with idolatry. For the connection between groves and idolatry in the Bible see, for example: Deuteronomy 16.21; Judges 3.7.

Plate 11: The Blossom.

> Merry Merry Sparrow
> Under leaves so green
> A happy Blossom
> Sees you swift as arrow
> Seek your cradle narrow
> Near my Bosom.
>
> Pretty Pretty Robin
> Under leaves so green
> A happy Blossom
> Hears you sobbing sobbing
> Pretty Pretty Robin
> Near my Bosom.

The simple lyric with its remarkable illustration has occasioned considerable debate. Wicksteed's interpretation includes a sexual allegory: 'The birds are the male element as seen by the maiden'; the 'illustration is a poetic and symbolic rendering of the phallus prone and erect, a pillar of vegetable flame breaking at the crest into mulitudinous life of many happy spirits, one of which finds its home in the lap of the happy mother'.[1] Hirsch interprets the poem as an allegory of the soul's imprisonment in the body.[2] Such divergence of interpretation reflects in part the indeterminacy of Blake's language: the ambiguous syntax makes firm distinctions impossible. Are the birds or the blossom or both 'Under leaves so green'? Is the speaker to be identified with the blossom or not? The poem can be construed in several different ways, and the relatively abstract design allows a comparable latitude.

In the poems of Innocence, joy and weeping are closely related. Weeping is an expression of joy (plate 4). Both are associated with protective love (plates 16–17, 20–21, 25), and with the vision of a personal saviour (plates 8, 12, 13–14, 18, 26, 27). The speakers of Innocence do not separate pain from pleasure, or discomfort from happiness; like the Chimney Sweeper of the next poem, who is 'cold' *and* 'warm', or the Little Black Boy, who sees love in the burning heat of the sun, they can reconcile opposites joyfully. The Blossom that is happy as it sees the merry Sparrow and as it hears the sobbing Robin, shows a typical sense of the relatedness of contrasting aspects of life.[3] The colouring of the design also brings opposites together. In the flame-like form that rises from grass up the right-hand side of the plate, and sends a side shoot underneath the text, warm and cold hues mingle harmoniously: blue, crimson, purple and violet. This emblematic blossom is brightened with streaks of gold and outlined in black. Naked, winged cherubs sport within its upper curves: one sits reading a book or paper, two embrace, two converse in flight. A sixth (with no wings visible) has arms raised as if in joy. Among them sits an angelic mother, winged, golden-haloed, attending to an infant in her lap. The white sun behind her recalls the shepherd's halo on the previous plate. The illustration seems related in its lines and colouring to that of plate 18 'The Divine Image', in which contrasting elements are shown to spring from the same root, identified with the divine love of the saviour.

The title is gold, and there are gold highlights on some of the cherubs' wings, and on the mother's wings and shoulder. The border is composed of simple vines which sprout four tiny leaves at the top, and meet in a curl.

[1] Wicksteed, *Blake's Innocence and Experience*, pp. 125–6.

[2] Hirsch, *Innocence and Experience*, pp. 181–4.

[3] In the Bible the sparrow is seen as protected by divine care: Psalm 84.3, 'the sparrow has found a house, and the swallow a nest for herself, where she may lay her young, even thine altar'; see also Matt. 10.29. The Robin is traditionally associated with pity and with calvary: it is said to have picked a thorn out of Christ's crown, and was stained with His blood. In 'Who killed Cock Robin?' the sparrow is an archer, the robin his victim.

Plate 12: The Chimney Sweeper

When my mother died I was very young,
And my father sold me while yet my tongue,
Could scarcely cry weep weep weep weep,
So your chimneys I sweep & in soot I sleep.

Theres little Tom Dacre. who cried when his head
That curl'd like a lambs back, was shav'd, so I said.
Hush Tom never mind it, for when your head's bare,
You know that the soot cannot spoil your white hair

And so he was quiet. & that very night.
As Tom was a sleeping he had such a sight,
That thousands of sweepers Dick, Joe, Ned & Jack
Were all of them lock'd up in coffins of black,

And by came an Angel who had a bright key
And he open'd the coffins & set them all free.
Then down a green plain leaping laughing they run
And wash in a river and shine in the Sun.

Then naked & white, all their bags left behind.
They rise upon clouds, and sport in the wind.
And the Angel told Tom, if he'd be a good boy,
He'd have God for his father & never want joy.

And so Tom awoke and we rose in the dark
And got with our bags & our brushes to work.
Tho' the morning was cold, Tom was happy & warm
So if all do their duty, they need not fear harm.

[151]

The young sweep of this song reveals the grim facts of his existence without anger or condemnation, although the implications of his account for the contemporary reader are clear ('So your chimneys I sweep').[1] His tale contrasts with the idyllic pastoral vision of poems like 'The Lamb' and 'The Shepherd'. It is not only the absence of loving care in the city that is exposed here: the shaving of Tom Dacre's head 'That curl'd like a lambs back' may remind us that sheep are bred to be fleeced.[2] Like the Little Black Boy's faith, Tom's dream is conditioned by his environment.[3] But whereas the Black Boy learns in the light of maternal love, Tom learns in fear and deprivation: he sees his mortal existence as a form of death, and in his vision divine love is a reward for obedience.[4] Although faith brings a triumph over misery, the poem's final line seems disconcerting. The sweep may appear naive to the experienced eye, which sees that Tom's Angel would give comfort to those with an interest in keeping down the price of chimney sweeping.[5]

The text, which is hard to read, is covered by a wash of blue, grey, yellow and pink, to form a smokey sky. The murky impression is relieved at the bottom by the brightening horizon and by the clear blue of the river. Here an angelic figure with a dark blue halo and a flowing robe bends down to help a naked child climb out of a black coffin. To the left, eleven other naked boys celebrate their liberty on the green river bank. The boys have gold highlights, and sport on a fine line of gold. Golden rays shine from the angel's robe, more gold is seen faintly around his halo. The tree that rises from bottom right beside and behind the text has two tiny figures (scarcely visible) in a fork opposite stanza 4. Other figures appear in and around the title: in the 'C' a minute sweep bending under his sack can just be distinguished; three figures appear dimly above 'Sweeper', and another to the right of the 'r'.[6] The title is gold, there are gold highlights on the vine in the left margin, and on the tree at the right.

At the top of the border, a vine forms three loops and hangs over each corner into a flower bell. Opposite the last stanza, reed-like leaves bend their heads downwards. The one on the left has a tip like an arrow head. Elsewhere in the *Songs* similar arrow heads are associated with self-protection, with an 'arming' of the emotions which imprisons the individual (see plate 41). Here, the image may illuminate the sweep's reconciliation of joy with duty.

[1] In line 2 'weep' suggests both the sweeper's 'cry' and the child's crying. In 1788 an attempt had been made to improve the conditions endured by children apprenticed to master sweeps. Porter's Act was intended to set the minimum age at eight; to limit the hours of work; to ensure that sweepers were properly washed every week; and to stop the use of children in chimneys on fire. (In the event the Act was not implemented.) The background is discussed by Erdman, *Prophet Against Empire*, p. 132, and Nurmi in 'Fact and Symbol in "The Chimney Sweeper" of Blake's *Songs of Innocence*,' *Blake: A Collection of Critical Essays*, edited by Northrop Frye (Englewood Cliffs, New Jersey, 1966), pp. 15–22.

[2] Gardner suggests that 'Tom Dacre is a foundling's name', derived from the Lady Ann Dacre's Alms Houses in Blake's Westminster: Stanley Gardner, *Blake* (London, 1968), pp. 78–9.

[3] Like the Little Black Boy's faith, Tom's may reflect Blake's reading of Swedenborg. Kathleen Raine cites a passage from *Concerning the Earth's in our Solar System*, in which spirits called 'Sweepers of Chimnies' cast off their dark raiment when called by angels, and become shining angels themselves. See *Blake and Tradition*, I, 25–6. Also Glen, *Vision and Disenchantment*, pp. 99–102.

[4] The traditional spiritual values of black and white have become associated with the two masters – earthly and divine – he now serves.

[5] David Fuller says of the sweepers' faith 'It is what such a religion always is: . . . real in its effects upon the sufferer though false in its claims about the world'. *Blake's Heroic Argument* (Beckenham, 1988), p. 78.

[6] In other copies, as Erdman notes (*IB* 53), one of the three figures above 'Sweeper' 'waves his sweeps brush in the air', and 'At line 13, above "Angel" a small figure holds out the handle end of a key'. These details are not visible here.

Plate 13: The Little Boy lost

Father, father, where are you going
O do not walk so fast.
Speak father, speak to your little boy
Or else I shall be lost,

The night was dark no father was there
The child was wet with dew.
The mire was deep, & the child did weep
And away the vapour flew

Like the previous poem, this song and its sequel focus on a parentless child, and on the faith that springs from loss.[1] The compressed narrative and the illustrations are highly ambiguous. In the first stanza of 'The Little Boy lost' the child's anxiety is expressed but not explained. The second stanza confirms his isolation and danger, but leaves uncertainty about its cause (does 'no father was there' mean that the father has left the child, or that the child has been led astray by an illusion, or both?). The illustration reduces without fully resolving the ambiguity: the boy, in a white gown and narrow-brimmed hat, reaches after a mysterious flame of marsh fire that shines in the darkness. The elaborate colouring creates a soft, misty, dream-like atmosphere (the child's gown is like a nightshirt). The white triangle of the flame, partially outlined in grey, has a halo of pale mauve, yellow and blue, in which rays of gold appear. Triangular shadows, alternating with more gold rays, push out from the halo into the dull blue of the night sky. The green at the boy's feet is lit with gold. The tree behind bends over him, its leafless branch echoing the lines of his outstretched arms. Between the boy and the tree trunk, fine black outlines suggest bulrushes.

Following the lead of Wicksteed, a number of critics have interpreted the poem as an allegory in which, as Keynes says, 'the child represents the human spirit seeking the conventional "God", or Father, promised to our childish minds, but proving to be non-existent as we flounder in the mire of the material world'.[2] Although such a specific explanation may seem reductive, some details here do point to the biblical understanding of God as a remote, mysterious and even cruel being. Allusions in the text associate the child with the desolation suffered by those who feel deserted or punished by the Lord. The mire is an image of such desolation; the outcast Nebuchadnezzar is repeatedly described as 'wet with dew of heaven'.[3] The bulrushes and the fire in the illustration may evoke the history of Moses, who was abandoned amid bulrushes, and led through the wilderness by a pillar of fire at night.[4] Such hints suggest that the song is not the first part of a moral fable, but defines a spiritual state that is a prelude to redemption.

The lower part of the plate is lighter and warmer, and offers intimations of the spiritual comfort that is rarely absent for long in the world of Innocence. The faintly printed text seems to have been partly retouched in grey, and has a pleasantly variegated appearance. It is guarded by six angels in flowing grey gowns, one standing either side of each stanza, two flying without wings in a light blue sky beneath. The one at top left, who reaches a hand to the 'T' of the title, may be male. The others are female. The title is brightened with gold.[5] A tiny figure sits on the 'L' of 'Little' (perhaps playing on a pipe), another, scarcely visible, lies along the 'B' of 'Boy', a third sits with arm raised in the lower loop of the same letter, while a swan – an emblem of good fortune, as Baine points out – is seen behind the rest of the word.[6] Fine stems with tiny leaves flourish around the title and between the stanzas, while vines coil and curve at the bottom (the vine between the flying angels has gold highlights; so have the angels). Two indistinct birds fly upwards beneath the title, another to the right of 'fast' has become a blur; a bulrush arches over a fourth bird at top right. The lower part of the border is composed of green bulrushes, three

[153]

either side; in the top half thin reeds lean out, and curl around the corners of the plate. Grey lines at the bottom suggest water.

1 An early version of this poem was included in *An Island in the Moon*. See Introduction.

2 Wicksteed, *Blake's Innocence and Experience*, p. 105. Geoffrey Keynes, *Blake: Songs of Innocence and of Experience* (London, 1970), plate 13.

3 See Job 30.19, Psalm 69.2, and the trials of Nebuchadnezzar, Daniel 4.15,23,25; 5.21.

4 The rush is proverbially associated with mire (Job 8.11). Friar Rush is another name for the Will-'o-the-Wisp or marsh fire.

5 Wicksteed notes that small initial letters in 'lost' of this title, and in 'found' of the next poem's title, indicates that Blake intended the two songs to form one poem: *Blake's Innocence and Experience*, p. 105. See note 5 on next poem.

6 Rodney M. Baine, with the assistance of Mary R. Baine, *The Scattered Portions* (Athens, Georgia, 1986), p. 55.

Plate 14: The Little Boy found

The little boy lost in the lonely fen,
Led by the wand'ring light,
Began to cry, but God ever nigh,
Appeard like his father in white.

He kissed the child & by the hand led
And to his mother brought,
Who in sorrow pale. thro' the lonely dale
Her little boy weeping sought.

The poem shows that distress and faith are intimately related. We have already seen that weeping has an important place in the vision of Innocence (see plate 11). Here the weeping child is immediately comforted, and so eventually is his weeping mother. In this respect the poem is like 'The Chimney Sweeper': both show that 'The Lord is nigh unto them that are of a broken heart' (Psalm 34.18). There is a characteristic ambiguity in the statement 'God . . . Appeared like his father in white'. Has the father returned, to be transfigured in the grateful eyes of the child?[1] Or has the saviour taken the appearance – and the place – of the father?[2] In either case, God is seen in a loving human form which contrasts with the remote and mysterious divinity alluded to in the first song.[3]

The illustration above the text is sharper (less misty) and warmer than that on the previous plate. The haloed adult who leads the child by the hand between massive tree trunks could be either male or female: the long flowing fair hair and high-waisted gown leave the gender undetermined. Is it the saviour or the mother who leads the child? The uncertainty may suggest a widening of the child's identification of loving saviour with loving parent.[4] The adult's glowing russet halo illuminates the dull blue-brown night sky with golden rays. The brim of the child's hat also looks like a halo. There are streaks of gold on the green earth at the feet of the figures, and golden highlights on the tree at far left.

In the right margin below, a wingless angel, apparently female, floats with arms outstretched, gown billowing behind. A curling vine-like form issues from the 'y' of 'Boy', winding along the top of the text; another goes down the left margin; a third grows beside the text at the bottom. The title, which puts out streamers, is partly filled with gold (there is none on the first 'e' or the last five letters of 'Little').[5]

The illustration does not fill the plate, leaving a white margin at top and sides. In the top margin a green zig-zag pattern has been added, which terminates in the side margins after one or two strokes. At the right a single brown triangle appears. The border is a simple green frame, which curves up as if from the monumental base and is broken at either side of the illustrations by a scroll and leaf form.

[1] God's white appearance associates him with the transfigured Christ: Matthew 17.2; Luke 9.27. In 'The Divine Image' we learn that the 'father' appears wherever there is love: 'Mercy Pity Peace and Love / Is God our father dear'.

[2] Keynes, concluding his interpretation of both poems, suggests that in this plate 'man has been restored to the life of the imagination and thereby saved' (ibid, plate 14). Wicksteed says 'I feel sure that the boy's restoration to his mother symbolises the Return to Earth which the illumination of Vision brings about' (ibid, p. 107).

[3] In the second case, the vision of the saviour not only makes a hostile world endurable, it actually mends matters. In this view, the two 'Little Boy' songs present the theme of redemption in the form of a fairy tale. Larrissy comments on this and comparable poems in Innocence: 'such innocent imaginings are both witness to the possibility of loving community and severly limited misunderstandings of the world': Edward Larrissy, *William Blake* (Oxford, 1975), p. 28.

[4] Keynes suggests that the adult 'may be one of Blake's not infrequent androgynous figures, having both mother and father attributes' (ibid).

[5] Erdman suggests that the first letter of 'found' is a swash capital (*IB* 55). I find Wicksteed's explanation more convincing here (see previous plate, note 5).

Plate 15: Laughing Song,

When the green woods laugh with the voice of joy
And the dimpling stream runs laughing by,
When the air does laugh with our merry wit,
And the green hill laughs with the noise of it.

When the meadows laugh with lively green
And the grasshopper laughs in the merry scene.
When Mary and Susan and Emily.
With their sweet round mouths sing Ha, Ha, He.

When the painted birds laugh in the shade
Where our table with cherries and nuts is spre[ad]
Come live & be merry and join with me,
To sing the sweet chorus of Ha, Ha, He.

An early version of this poem was inscribed in a copy of *Poetical Sketches*, where it is attributed to 'a Young Shepherd' (see Introduction). The invitation 'Come live & be merry and join with me' recalls Marlowe's famous lyric 'Come live with me and be my love', but here the various pastoral delights are seen as participating in the pleasure of the beholder. The emphasis falls on communal joy rather than on individual appetite: laughter is shared enjoyment which, like song, draws various voices into one harmony.[1]

The design gives a little more emphasis to the erotic aspect of the invitation.[2] If the tone of the lyric suggests a child-like innocence, the illustration above the text shows a group of young adults. David Bindman notes that this composition 'derives from Stothard's illustration to a *Drinking Song* in Ritson'.[3] Whether or not the table is spread with cherries and nuts, it is certainly spread with wine. The young man in pink, who stands barefooted with his back to the

[155]

reader, raises high a glass of wine in his right hand as if to lead the toast, and waves a white-plumed pink hat in his left as if to conduct the chorus. Six other figures, male and female are visible, seated around the table.[4] Their postures are relaxed, even languid. The group is unified visually by the surrounding green (supplied in part by the dense rectangular hedge or thicket in the background), and by the symmetrical composition. As in plates 6 and 7, the costume colours have been carefully balanced. The pink of the central figure adds to his prominence and (matching the wine) suggests the Bacchic nature of his joy. The grass near the figures' feet is streaked with gold, there is gold in the sky to the right of the hedge, and faint traces of gold in the hedge at top left.

There are several birds around the text, but fewer than in some other copies, as the printing is unclear. Most distinct are: one above 'Song' in the title, and another at top right of the text; the tiny one rising at top right of the third stanza; and three below the last stanza, one perched on a vine, another flying up to its left, a third flying downards below 'sing'. (Three flying below the vine here, and one below 'Ha, Ha,' have become indistinct blurs.) The title and the streamer to its right are filled with gold.

The elaborate pattern of the border is apparently made by wings at the top and sides, with vaguely sketched heads. The wings seem angelic, but the head at the top may be a bat's. In his designs for Edward Young's *Night Thoughts* Blake painted a winged bat, presiding over a Bacchic celebration, to illustrate Young's lines on thoughtless merriment, 'a mere Froth of Joy'.[5] The border may thus be intended to qualify the festive mood of the poem. In copy E of the *Songs* this poem appears in both Innocence and Experience (see Introduction).

[1] Cf. Blake's annotations to Lavater: 'I hate scarce smiles I love laughing' (*E* 585; *K* 67).

[2] The chorus echoes a bawdy love song in *Troilus and Cressida* III, i:

> Yet that which seems to wound to kill
> Doth turn oh oh to ha ha he

[3] *Blake as an Artist*, pp. 59–60.

[4] The grey object to the right of the woman in violet looks like a feather fan. In some copies it is another figure. See *IB* 56.

[5] See *William Blake's Designs for Edward Young's 'Night Thoughts'*, edited by David V. Erdman, John E. Grant, Edward J. Rose, Michael Tolley, 2 vols (Oxford, 1980), II, 2 vols, *NT* 409, 410. Bat wings are usually associated with the 'Spectre' of abstract reason in Blake's work.

Plates 16–17: A Cradle Song

Sweet dreams form a shade,
O'er my lovely infants head.
Sweet dreams of pleasant streams,
By happy silent moony beams

Sweet sleep with soft down.
Weave thy brows an infant crown.
Sweet sleep Angel mild,
Hover o'er my happy child.

Sweet smiles in the night,
Hover over my delight.
Sweet smiles Mothers smiles
All the livelong night beguiles.

Sweet moans, dovelike sighs,
Chase not slumber from thy eyes,
Sweet moans. sweeter smiles,
All the dovelike moans beguiles.

Sleep sleep happy child,
All creation slept and smil'd.
Sleep sleep, happy sleep.
While o'er thee thy mother weep

Sweet babe in thy face,
Holy image I can trace.
Sweet babe once like thee.
Thy maker lay and wept for me

Wept for me for thee for all,
When he was an infant small.
Thou his image ever see.
Heavenly face that smiles on thee,

Smiles on thee on me on all,
Who became an infant small,
Infant smiles are his own smiles,
Heaven & earth to peace beguiles.

This is one of the longest of the Innocence poems in this copy – with 'Night' and 'On Another's Sorrow'. It appears to be modelled on Watts's *A Cradle Hymn*, in which an infant is told how the Son of God 'became a child'. As Pinto says, Watts's poem 'is classical in its clarity, its logical development and its sharp outlines,' and it develops a contrast between the human child and the Saviour.[1] Blake's poem tends to dissolve clear distinctions in order to suggest the union of the human and the divine. The song is a fine example of Blake's expressive use of sound: the repetitions, internal rhymes, soft consonents, long vowels and subtle rhythms create a powerful incantatory effect. The singing mother does not develop an argument; instead she weaves a kind of spell. Her vision of the Angel hovering over her crowned infant evokes traditional images of the nativity even before she draws an explicit parallel between her child and its 'maker'. As in 'The Lamb', separate identities are unified: the 'Holy image' is traced in the child's face; the 'Heavenly face' that smiles on the child is at once the mother's and the maker's. The familiar domestic situation can be seen as a kind of incarnation, in which divine love appears in human form. The final reference to smiles that beguile 'Heaven & earth to peace' recalls Milton's ode 'On the Morning of Christ's Nativity', where the birth of Christ is accompanied by a divine harmony which

> alone
> Could hold all heaven and earth in happier union
> (107–8)

Despite the reassuring emphasis on love and security, the references to the beguiling effect of smiles and peace is mildly disturbing, as it suggests the illusory nature of the seductive mood that is established. A similar ambivalence appears in the designs. Visually there is a vivid contrast between the first and second plates. Apart from the difference in the space allowed for illustration, the two plates present a contrast between natural images of flourishing, untrammelled growth, and a static domestic interior.

On the first plate, the wandering, streamy leaves and stems in the margins may suggest the 'shade' of sleep. The eye is drawn down by the mazy forms to discover tiny figures who sit, sleep or fly among them. The gilded title sports three minute beings: a piper (just visible) leaning against the first 'A', a figure with knees drawn up inside the 'C', another standing in the 'D'. More can be seen in the margins: to the left a female lifts one arm by stanza 2 (perhaps an angel of sleep); by stanza 3 two infants appear with arms raised; by stanza 5 a figure huddles beneath the branches of a tree; by stanza 6 a robed figure stands reaching up (perhaps the 'Holy image' raising a lamp?). To the right, on the foliage that sprouts from between stanzas 1 and 2, a figure sits hunched up; immediately below, someone in a flowing white gown lies as if asleep (with head towards the left). By stanza 4 a figure walks on a curling leaf. The vegetation opposite the fifth and sixth stanzas has some golden highlights. At the bottom right corner a head of ripe grain is just visible.[2] The contrasting rhythms of leaves, fronds and vines, blend easily together here. The decorations combine images of profuse, unchecked growth with intimations of a protective order. The border is a simple rectangular frame at the top (with crossed fronds at top centre). At either side the sides five scrolls appear, then a vine with leaves. Along the bottom a pair of sweeping scroll forms are joined by crossed strands (echoing the pattern at the top).

The scene in the second plate resembles Renaissance paintings of the Madonna and Child.[3] The colouring associates the interior with the exterior scenes of Innocence. The green of the background screen echoes the protective trees or hedges of 6 and 15, while the centrally placed blue of the mother's full dress may recall the piper of plate 2. The carpet and furniture add warmth to the scene. The cradle has gold along the rim and inside the top of its hood; the curling frame of the chair shines with gold. Around the sleeping child's head the pillow appears like a white halo. If the composition emphasizes the security and love enjoyed by the child, this impression is complicated by other elements of the design. In contrast to the free-flowing stems and fibres of the previous plate, this scene is dominated by woven objects: carpet, screen, clothing, bed linen. The mother's hair appears to be covered by a light scarf. The wicker of the child's cradle has been carefully emphasized. In this context the unusual prominence given to woven objects may suggest the danger inherent in material security, the possibility of spiritual constraint or entrapment (in the song weaving is seen as a function of sleep).[4] The design seems closely related to that of plate 48, which illustrates 'Infant Sorrow' (where the child strives in vain against its 'swaddling bands'). The 'beguiling' nature of the mother's vision of peace is again suggested.[5]

At the top of the plate, curving stems grow around the stanzas, spreading leaves into the right margin. In the left margin, by stanza 1, a mother stands with a baby in her arms; a child runs towards stanza 2, while below (just visible) a girl runs away. Beneath the text, there is gold at right and left. The border is formed of hanging drapery, outlined in grey-brown and shading to black at the bottom.

[1] See Vivian De Sola Pinto, 'William Blake, Isaac Watts, and Mrs Barbauld', in *The Divine Vision: Studies in the Poetry and Art of William Blake*, edited by Vivian De Sola Pinto (London, 1957), 67–87, p. 77.

[2] Two more heads of grain and three tiny figures that appear in other copies are indistinguishable here (see *IB* 57).

[3] Bindman compares the image to Raphael's *Madonna di Loretto, Blake as an Artist*, p. 60; Leader compares it with Bellini's *The Madonna of the Meadows* in the National Gallery, *Reading Blake's Songs*, p. 43.

[4] David Wagenknecht comments 'If the infant suggests to us the Christ-child, Blake has most unpleasantly reminded us of his dependence upon the flesh in his incarnate condition'. *Blake's Night: William Blake and the Idea of Pastoral* (Harvard University Press, Cambridge, Mass, 1973), p. 72.

[5] In Milton's Ode the peace at the nativity is shown to be in a sense beguiling, as it heralds a continuation of the trials of fallen history: the 'wakeful trump of doom' (l. 156) must sound before heaven and

earth can be truly unified. In Blake's *Europe* the incarnation is succeeded by a sleep of 'Eighteen hundred years', in which human destiny is ruled by a dreaming mother goddess, before the apocalyptic awakening of the French Revolution. The 'sleep' of creation is referred to in 'The Little Girl Lost' in Experience, where it is associated with a fall which separates earth from her 'maker' (plate 34).

Plate 18: The Divine Image.

> To Mercy Pity Peace and Love.
> All pray in their distress:
> And to these virtues of delight
> Return their thankfulness.
>
> For Mercy Pity Peace and Love,
> Is God our father dear:
> And Mercy Pity Peace and Love,
> Is Man his child and care.
>
> For Mercy has a human heart
> Pity, a human face:
> And Love, the human form divine,
> And Peace, the human dress.
>
> Then every man of every clime,
> That prays in his distress,
> Prays to the human form divine
> Love Mercy Pity Peace,
>
> And all must love the human form.
> In heathen, turk or jew,
> Where Mercy, Love & Pity dwell,
> There God is dwelling too.

This song defines the essence of humanity and divinity in terms that include no reference to reason or justice. In looking beyond the forms that distinguish different creeds, to the human form that unites them, it works against the divisive assumptions of more orthodox Christian writers such as Isaac Watts. In 'Praise for the Gospel' Watts wrote:

> Lord, I ascribe it to thy Grace
> And not to Chance, as others do,
> That I was born of *Christian* Race,
> And not a *Heathen*, or a *Jew*.[1]

Blake's song not only asserts that all creeds have the same emotional basis, but implies that all are essentially Christian. Its view of the relationship between humanity and divinity is comparable to that in I John 4.16: 'God is love; and he that dwelleth in love dwelleth in God, and God in him'.[2] As in other poems of Innocence, the human and the divine are seen as one.

The delicately coloured illustration that surrounds the text may allude to John 15, where Jesus identifies himself as the true vine, and explains that those who do not abide in him are cast forth as withered branches 'into the fire' (v. 6). Blake's stylized design apparently revises this notion: here the vine encircles a serpentine, flame-like form which seems both exuberant and protective. In a vision where Mercy Pity Peace and Love prevail, there can be no casting out. The flame begins like a blue fountain, but the blue soon combines with crimson and purple. The colouring, with its gold highlights, recalls that of 'The Blossom' on plate 11. At the top, within the shelter of the final curve, two wingless angels of mercy, both female, respond swiftly to a pair of children kneeling with hands and faces raised in prayer. The angel who walks carries a round object under her right arm and a pitcher in her left hand (Hirsch suggests these are bread and wine).[3] Both comforters have been partially reinforced in ink, whereas the children remain rather indistinct. The flame leads the eye down the page to the white-robed figure of the saviour, who stands between fire and vine as if growing from their common root. His white halo is surrounded by blue, and sends out rays of blue and gold into the yellow of the sky. His left arm reaches out to touch the hand of a naked man, who rises from the flame. The indistinct figure who reclines below is either naked or wearing a white robe, and has faint gold highlights on head and body. The gender of this figure is not determined here. In other copies it is female, which suggests that Blake's initial conception of the redeemer's role involved a healing of the breech between Adam and Eve, a reunification of the divided sexes. The diverse elements in the design all appear to spring ultimately from the same source, a source identified with the loving saviour.

The title is reinforced with gold. The border is composed of a green leafless vine at either side, which breaks into loops opposite the text. At the top the vines converge without meeting. At the bottom a broken black line provides a suggestion of roots.

[1] Isaac Watts, *Divine Songs*, p. 157.

[2] Blake quoted this verse from I John with approval in his annotations to Lavater (*E* 599; *K* 87).

[3] E. D. Hirsch, *Innocence and Experience*, p. 194.

Plate 19: Holy Thursday

Twas on a Holy Thursday their innocent faces clean
The children walking two & two in red & blue & gre[en]
Grey headed beadles walkd before with wands as white as snow
Till into the high dome of Pauls they like Thames waters flow

O what a multitude they seemd these flowers of London town
Seated in companies they sit with radiance all their own
The hum of multitudes was there but multitudes of lambs
Thousands of little boys & girls raising their innocent hands

Now like a mighty wind they raise to heaven the voice of song
Or like harmonious thunderings the seats of heaven among
Beneath them sit the aged men wise guardians of the poor
Then cherish pity, lest you drive an angel from your door

Unlike other poems of Innocence, this one refers to a particular event in a specific location.[1] The annual service of thanksgiving for charity-school children had been held at St. Paul's cathedral in London since 1782.[2] It was traditionally held on a Thursday but, Gardner notes, 'never took place either on Ascension Day or on Maunday Thursday, the two possible holy Thursdays of the church calendar'.[3] Blake's title apparently redefines the calendar, associating Christ's triumph with a communal celebration of pity. The children 'walking two & two in red & blue & green' may at first seem contained by the occasion – uniformed and regimented. This impression is reinforced by the illustrations above and below the text, which show the separate processions of the boys and the girls. At the top, the boys walk to the right in pairs behind two blue-coated beadles, one of whom has a 'wand'. The boys' uniforms of blue, green and red harmonise with the background as it shades from yellow to blue. At the bottom the girls move to the left, following in pairs a black-robed, white-haired matron or minister who carries a book, and who stands out starkly against the light background. Some of the girls have been redrawn, others are indistinct. Their blue or green dresses have gold highlights, and are set off by white aprons and caps. The design emphasizes the ceremonial nature of the event, in which children are *led* to their places. But the delighted response of the speaker in the poem soon makes the children appear to transcend all constraints. The similes and metaphors – 'Thames waters', 'flowers', 'radiance', 'multitudes of lambs' – introduce suggestions of natural abundance and energy, which reach a climax in the 'mighty wind' and 'harmonious thunderings' of the song. The description of the song evokes the resonance of St. Paul's dome and, as Malkin observed, recalls Revelation 19, which describes the celebration of the marriage of the Lamb (see *BR* 425–7). The last two lines may allude to one of the yearly hymns for charity children in the Wesleys' *Collection of Psalms and Hymns*, which compares the children's benefactors with divine guardians:

> With what resembling care and love
> Both worlds for us appear!
> Our friendly guardians, those above,
> Our benefactors here.[4]

The exuberant tone of the poem is to some extent modified by a sense of anticlimax, as the speaker's attention turns from the children to the 'aged men wise guardians of the poor' who sit beneath them. Other elements in the poem may also work against the mood of celebration. The 'guardians' and the 'Grey headed beadles . . . with wands as white as snow' are seen implicitly as shepherds of a multitude of lambs. Their stewardship may be compared with that of the shepherd of plate 5, whose care seems unconditional, who follows his flock, and whose own tongue shall be 'filled with praise'. The phrase 'seats of heaven' evokes a divinity that seems remote compared with the 'Divine Image' of the previous poem, or with the 'maker' celebrated in 'The Lamb' and 'A Cradle Song'. The voices which rise like 'harmonious thunderings' among those 'seats' sound vaguely threatening, and in this respect seem quite unlike the joyful voices on plates 4, 6 or 15. Such comparisons may give rise to unsettling questions. Do the children's voices shake the establishment of heaven? Does the poem expose the moral complacency of those who make a public display of charity? But if such questions arise, they don't negate the speaker's pleasure or the exuberant impression of innocence he creates.

The text is interlaced with tiny stems and leaves, some of which have been retouched (unlike the letters).[5] Beneath the first stanza, at the left, a barely visible stork flies; beneath the second, under the word 'innocent', a child sports with outstretched arms; beneath the third, perched on a vine at the centre, an indistinct bird spreads its wings wide like an eagle (perhaps here an emblem of generosity).[6] The title is filled with gold, there is faint gold in the leaves to left and right of the title, in those beneath 'DAY' of the title, in the scrolls of foliage above the girls' heads, and on the left wing of the eagle.

The border is more elaborate than usual. From the brown rectangular base sprout grey and brown leaves which curl over like fingers at either side of the girls. Above these grey leafless vines wind up to meet three brown scrolls, a fourth curling over the top corner. The border is dominated by the winged, oval ring at top centre. In *Jerusalem* plate 33[37] a winged disc is associated with the divine mercy that supports Albion in his fallen condition. Here the emblem apparently suggests the divinity inherent in acts of pity.[7]

---

[1] An early version of this song appeared in *An Island on the Moon*, see Introduction. Wicksteed notes that its diction is less child-like than that of other Innocence poems: *Blake's Innocence and Experience*, p. 103.

[2] The charity school children's anniversary procession had been a popular event since the beginning of the eighteenth century. See M. G. Jones, *The Charity School Movement* (Cambridge, 1938), 59–61.

[3] Stanley Gardner, *Blake's 'Innocence' and 'Experience' Retraced* (London and New York, 1986), p. 35.

[4] *A Collection of Psalms and Hymns*, edited by John Wesley and Charles Wesley, tenth edition (London, 1779), p. 55. Glen notes that the injunction in the last line echoes Hebrews 13.2 'Be not forgetful to entertain strangers: for thereby some have entertained angels unawares': *Vision and Disenchantment*, pp. 120–8.

[5] In some copies a flame rises between the words of the title (see *IB* 60). Here it appears as a leaf.

[6] Baine notes that the eagle was associated with generosity (among many other virtues) by the emblem writers: *The Scattered Portions*, p. 73.

[7] See Raine's discussion of the 'sacred heirogram' of the winged disc, *Blake and Tradition*, II, 261.

Plates 20–21: Night

The sun descending in the west.
The evening star does shine.
The birds are silent in their nest,
And I must seek for mine,
The moon like a flower,
In heavens high bower;
With silent delight,
Sits and smiles on the night.

Farewell green fields and happy groves,
Where flocks have took delight;
Where lambs have nibbled, silent moves
The feet of angels bright;
Unseen they pour blessing,
And joy without ceasing,
On each bud and blossom,
And each sleeping bosom.

They look in every thoughtless nest
Where birds are coverd warm;
They visit caves of every beast,
To keep them all from harm;
If they see any weeping,
That should have been sleeping
They pour sleep on their head
And sit down by their bed.

When wolves and tygers howl for prey
They pitying stand and weep;
Seeking to drive their thirst away,
And keep them from the sheep.
But if they rush dreadful;
The angels most heedful,
Recieve each mild spirit.
New worlds to inherit.

And there the lions ruddy eyes,
Shall flow with tears of gold;
And pitying the tender cries,
And walking round the fold:
Saying: wrath by his meekness
And by his health, sickness.
Is driven away,
From our immortal day.

And now beside thee bleating lamb.
I can lie down and sleep;
Or think on him who bore thy name.
Grase after thee and weep.
For wash'd in lifes river.
My bright mane for ever.
Shall shine like the gold.
As I guard o'er the fold.

The need for divine protection at night is a familiar theme in eighteenth-century hymns.[1] Charles Wesley's 'All praise to him who dwells in bliss' is fairly typical in its imagery and argument:

Whom thou dost guard, O King of kings
No evil shall molest;
Under the shadow of Thy wings
Shall they securely rest.

Thy angels shall around their beds
Their constant stations keep;
Thy faith and truth shall shield their heads,
For thou dost never sleep.[2]

Blake's poem makes use of comparable imagery in a pastoral context that relates the ministry of angels to the protective role of the shepherd. In its progress from a celebration of natural harmony to a vision of 'new worlds', the song exposes and attempts to resolve a contradiction between two ideas of divine benevolence: one traditionally associated with the good shepherd who must protect his lambs from the lion and the wolf, the other with the divine maker who cares for all his creatures.[3] The first two stanzas establish a mood of universal peace and contentment, but the pastoral idyll is modified in stanza three as the speaker's vision expands to include 'caves of every beast'.[4] The impossibility of establishing universal peace in this world is recognized in the fourth stanza: the angels seek to drive away the natural 'thirst' of beasts of prey, but may fail; they seek to guard the sheep, but may fail. In these 'green fields and happy groves', apparently, their benevolent intentions are hardly realized beyond the comfort of sleep. But the speaker's faith is sustained by the vision of 'new worlds' in which natural conflicts are resolved, a vision that recalls Isaiah 11.6 and Revelation 22.1–5.[5] As in other poems of Innocence, the distinctions between separate identities dissolve as the lion identifies itself with both the shepherd and the lamb.

The song shows how faith triumphs over its own awareness of contradictions. In doing so, however, it draws attention to the limits of natural harmony, and of divine protection on earth. The speaker's vision of new worlds, in which individual identity is liberated from sickness and wrath, has a powerful emotional appeal. But one may wonder whether the transformation of the lion into a pitying herbivore reveals the lion's true identity, or conveniently disposes of it.

The design of the first plate shows a landscape in which angelic forms are seen visiting and protecting under a night sky. This plate has an outstandingly delicate finish, although particular details remain unclear. The original red-brown print colour has been almost entirely painted over with pale yellow ochre, and the rest of the colouring creates a soft, dream-like atmosphere. The tall, slender tree that rises up the right-hand margin, and curls gracefully around the title at the top, has feathery leaves. A vine coils gently around its trunk. At the foot of the tree a large golden animal appears in the mouth of a cave hollowed in a green hill. The animal's features are indistinct: in other copies it appears as a lion (*IB* 61). Above the hill a tiny winged figure flies towards the tree from the left, as if to bring comfort to the beast in its cave. Higher up, beside stanza 1, two white stars shine either side of the tree, and two indistinct yellow birds perch on a branch. Higher still, a winged, golden angel with a white halo sits within a fork of the tree with head bowed as if reading, and in the fork above another one stands, carrying something white (a book or paper?) in its right hand.

The left-hand margin has several angelic beings, all golden. A robed figure at the bottom holds a dark staff in his right hand (or raises an arm in silhouette to reach a dark object above). Above, there are several intimations of cosmic harmony, as celestial beings sport among the stars. A second robed angel with tiny butterfly wings holds up its right arm to a scarcely visible golden orb (to the right of which four dim stars appear). The orb is partly obscured by the trailing robe of a third angel above, who flies with arms raised, while a smaller winged angel hovers overhead. Four white stars shine out beside lines 5 and 6, and another golden orb appears beside line 4. In the foreground a stream runs between green banks (the nearside bank is almost invisible). The text has been carefully retouched in gold. The title, and the streamers that come from it, are gold.

The intimations of peace and security here are modified by the border. At the top, the squat

[163]

brown head of a bat is seen, its outstretched wings revealing two sections of their webbing at either side of the title space. Faint grey and gold serpentine forms twine around the lower corners and up the sides level with third stanza. The sides of the bat wings and the border below are lined in gold, as are the serpentine forms at bottom. Blake used the image of encompassing wings to suggest the cover of darkness at night in his *Night Thoughts* designs (see 'raven winged Darkness' NT 94). But bat wings usually have negative connotations in his work: they are associated with intellectual darkness (see plate 15), and with the abstract reasoning power of the 'Spectre' (*Jerusalem* 6, 33). If the poem suggests a triumph of faith over fear, the border may suggest that this vision is a rationalization of fear.

The second plate contrasts with the first in its finish: it has a slightly harder quality, as in the heavy shading of the tree, and particulars are seen more distinctly (for example, the carefully painted stars). In the right margin, in the dark blue of the sky, four stars shine (three are five-pointed), and dense green foliage hangs down in cloud-like forms. In the left margin stands a tree which carries two indistinct angel forms (by stanzas 1 and 3) both touched with gold. To the right of the tree a black stem rises, flanked by vague brown foliage.[6] On the grass are five young women in white robes. Behind the two at the right a huge moon rises to make a halo for both. The three walking at the left have gold highlights in their robes; their haloes merge into a white gold-rimmed cloud. The one at the right of this group holds a lyre in her left hand. Perhaps, as Wagenknecht suggests (55) the figures represent the five senses, here seen as divine and innocent rather than as the origin of selfish appetite. The grass on which they walk glows with traces of gold. On the horizon at right, brown patches may indicate distant dwellings. In the foreground a stream runs by. The border in dull green is a simple frame, with the suggestion of a base at bottom, and a single scroll at either side of the first stanza.

[1] The opening of this hymn has been compared to Mrs Barbauld's Hymn V (see Pinto, *The Divine Vision*, p. 85; Nick Shripton, 'William Blake: Hell's Hymnbook', p. 27). Holloway compares the poem to Doddridge's Hymn 100: John Holloway, *Blake: The Lyric Poetry* (London, 1968), p. 35. See also Watts's 'An Evening Song', *Divine Songs*, pp. 246–7. For a detailed examination of the poems's relation to the pastoral tradition see Wagenknecht, *Blake's Night*, pp. 36–57.

[2] The hymn first appeared in the 1741 edition of the Wesleys' *A Collection of Psalms and Hymns*, under the title 'An Evening Hymn'.

[3] For the image of divinity as protector *from* wild beasts see John 10.11; as the protector *of* wild beasts, and all creatures, see Psalm 104 (especially vv. 20–22).

[4] Several critics have commented on the relationship between the mood and the stanza form of the poem. Ostriker notes that the alternation in each stanza between a ballad quatrain and four lines in anapestic dimeter produces 'a sensation of hovering between waking and dreaming': Alicia Ostriker, *Vision and Verse in William Blake* (Madison, 1966), p. 74. See also Leader, *Reading Blake's Songs*, p. 122.

[5] Glen notes that in the Swedenborgian doctrine with which Blake was familiar, 'night' and 'faith' were explicitly linked: 'Faith is called "night", because it receives light from charity, as the moon does from the sun; and therefore faith is also compared to the moon, and is called "the moon" ': *Vision and Disenchantment*, p. 141.

[6] In some copies this foliage appears as a St. Bernard's lily (as identified by Erdman, *IB* 62), but it is not identifiable here.

Sound the Flute!
Now it's mute.
Birds delight
Day and Night,
Nightingale
In the dale
Lark in Sky
Merrily
Merrily Merrily to welcome in the Year

Little Boy
Full of joy,

Little Girl
Sweet and small,
Cock does crow
So do you.
Merry voice
Infant noise
Merrily Merrily to welcome in the Year

Little Lamb
Here I am.
Come and lick
My white neck.
Let me pull
Your soft Wool.
Let me kiss
Your soft face
Merrily Merrily we welcome in the Year

With its lilting, dance-like rhythms, this song evokes a mood quite unlike the quiet joy of 'Night'. Here the lamb is embraced not in visionary 'New worlds', but in a natural world made new by the arrival of spring. Sound and silence, day and night, boy and girl become complementary elements in the rhythm and harmony of the song. The nightingale, traditionally associated with melancholy and evening, joins the lark of morning as a merry bird.[1] The 'infant noise' of the boy and girl, associated with the crowing cock, becomes the herald of a new dawn. The refrain might seem appropriate to a New Year or Christmas song ('Year' is capitalized). But here the year is shaped by the speaker's delight, not by the letter of the calendar. Spring is seen implicitly as an incarnation of divine joy (the words 'Here I am' which announce the speaker's presence to the lamb in the final stanza, are often used in the Bible to announce, or respond to, the presence of divinity).[2]

Bindman notes that the image of the mother with the naked child reaching out in the upper part of the first plate resembles the pastoral Madonnas of Titian.[3] Like the design on the second plate, it recalls the identification of the child and lamb shown on plate 8: parent and infant look down at a lamb and ewe, which look back up at them. An area of white sky to the left of the tree suggests the sun rising, but there is no twilight here – the scene is bright and sunny, with shade from the overhanging branches. The one discordant element is the woman's left hand which restrains the infant: carefully drawn in ink, it seems disproportionately large.

The colouring in the lower part of the plate also gives an impression of dawn. The angel sitting by stanza 1 plays a pipe, as if urging the vigorous growing forms around him into fruition. To the right above him a head of grass or ripening wheat is clearly visible (another immediately below, and one to the left of the catchword are scarcely distinguishable). A second angel reclines on a leaf near the words 'Little Boy'. Gold appears in many places on this plate: highlighting the fleeces of the sheep and the mother's red dress; glowing on the grass by the mother's hem; flecking the tree trunk; brightening the title and some of the leaves that sprout from it to the right and left, the curling stem at the left of the text, the two angels and the vegetation at the bottom. The border has two parts, echoing the design of the plate. Heads of ripening green wheat stand either side of the text area. A green vine stem forms three loops at top centre, and curves sinuously around the top corners and down either side towards the wheat.

On the second plate, the colouring of the text area creates another sunrise effect. The swirling stems in the right margin support heads of wheat: one (at top right) is a ripe brown; one beneath the lower angel and two at the right of the scene below are green. Both angels are lightly shaded with gold. Below the text the naked child embracing the lamb before two kneeling sheep has overcome the parental restraint shown on the first plate. The composition is related to the last plate of 'The Little Girl Found' in Experience, where children play with wild beasts. There is gold on the backs of the sheep, in the child's hair, on the grass below, in the yellow glow to the right, and in the serpentine streamer that plays over the water in the foreground. Coiling green tendrils form the top of the border. The sloping green lines at either side undulate at the bottom corners to give a suggestion of drapery; underneath they make vague foliage.

[1] For examples of the traditional association of the nightingale with melancholy and the lark with joy, see Milton's 'Il Penseroso' (51–62) and 'L'Allegro' (41–48).

[2] See for example Genesis 22.1, 11; 31.11; Exodus 3.4. Gleckner associates the shift in emphasis from sound in the first two stanzas to touch in the third with the theme of incarnation. Robert F. Gleckner, *The Piper and the Bard* (Detroit, 1959), p. 97.

[3] *Blake as an Artist*, p. 60.

Plate 24: Nurse's Song

When the voices of children are heard on the green
And laughing is heard on the hill,
My heart is at rest within my breast
And everything else is still

Then come home my children the sun is gone down
And the dews of night arise
Come come leave off play, and let us away
Till the morning appears in the skies

No no let us play, for it is yet day
And we cannot go to sleep
Besides in the sky, the little birds fly
And the hills are all coverd with sheep

Well well go & play till the light fades away
And then go home to bed
The little ones leaped & shouted & laugh'd
And all the hills ecchoed

As in 'The Ecchoing Green', the children's 'sports' in this song are used to draw attention to the passage of time. The dialogue between the nurse and the children in her care takes place on a temporal borderline – between the going down of the sun and the fading of the light – and brings two contrasting attitudes into focus. In the first stanza the voices and laughing of the children produce no equivalent animation in the nurse, but a sense of rest and stillness. If her mood suggests harmony, this impression is immediately shattered in the second stanza, where her concern about the oncoming night appears. The abrupt transition makes her initial contentment seem fragile and even illusory – a temporary release from care. In this context the fading of the light suggests the loss that comes with an adult awareness of consequences. In contrast, the harmony of the children has nothing to do with stillness or rest ('we cannot go to sleep'); the coming darkness casts no shadow over their present enjoyment; they are not set apart from the world, which echoes their joy.

The relationship between the nurse and the children seems at once close and remote, as she shares and is excluded from their pleasure. Her acquiescence in the last stanza indicates her increased sense of distance from them ('go home' replaces 'come home'). But the song and its final note of triumph are hers, and express her appreciation of their joy. A comparable ambivalence can be seen in the illustration below the text, in both the composition and the colouring. The nurse sits alone with her book while the children play as a group, but if she is apart she is not completely excluded. As Mary Lynne Johnson notes she is included in the visual circle formed by their game (the two children at the left hold out a handkerchief or scarf as an arch for the others to run through).[1] Between the gentle lines of the hills a yellow glow indicates the setting sun. Dark branches from the trees at left and right reach out over the figures towards a shadowy cloud, while other shadows gather at the edges of the picture. A dark frame is thus created around the grassy scene (relieved at the right by the lighter trunk of the slender, vine-encircled tree). The nurse has a light cap and collar, but her face is in shade, and her brown dress contributes to the darkness. Set against the outer darkness the pale blue and rose costumes of the children echo the colours of the sky. There is gold on the edge of the foreground hill, on the grass where the game proceeds, and in the sky, in fine streaks, below the line of the branches.

In contrast to the light and shade at the bottom of the plate, the upper portion has a watery appearance. The gold title blends with the flourishing blue and green foliage that surrounds it. Among the letters are several tiny figures, all hard to distinguish. A naked figure (just visible) clings to the first stroke of the 'N', another sits on a leaf at the end of the third stroke. One lunges head first through the 'u', another (perhaps robed) sits on the lower curve of the 'S' of 'Song' with a book in his lap, and at the top of the same letter a barely discernable figure supports a curling stem. Two recline on a leaf at the tail of the 'g'. To the right of the text, a tiny figure sits on a leaf by line 2, another by line 4 (both very faint in this copy).

In the right margin, a weeping willow droops into water, suggesting, perhaps, the sorrow that may soon displace present joy.[2] Stems and leaves grow between the stanzas, and some letters trail banner-like leaves. A vine loops and twists its way down the left-hand margin. Within the simple orange frame of the border, green lines rise and break into curves (some pushing out of the frame), then flame-like leaves appear and, higher up, curling vine tendrils which curve in a fork over the top corners.

[1] Mary Lynne Johnson's suggestion is reported by David Erdman (*IB* 65).

[2] The willow on plate 10, which shades the figures beneath it, is associated with the protective love of the saviour. This one offers no shade; Wicksteed sees it as 'a wonderfully expressive symbol of loving anxious care bending over Innocence', *Blake's Innocence and Experience*, p. 96.

Plate 25: Infant Joy

I have no name	Pretty joy!
I am but two days old.—	Sweet joy but two days old.
What shall I call thee?	Sweet joy I call thee;
I happy am	Thou dost smile,
Joy is my name.—	I sing the while
Sweet joy befall thee!	Sweet joy befall thee.

Like 'Spring', this song and its illustration present a natural delight in new life as an incarnation of divine joy. In the design the blossom and buds of brilliant crimson, outlined in black, stand out boldly against the pale sky. The figures within the opened petals enact an Adoration scene.[1] A mother in a blue dress nurses a baby in her lap, while a winged girl-angel stands with arms reaching out towards the infant. The angel is golden; the spot on her wing (barely visible in this copy) may identify her with the Greek goddess Psyche.[2] The petals of the flower seem protective, although those that curl over from the left may suggest containment, hinting perhaps at the potential constraints that face the new-born child. A comparable ambiguity appears in the song itself, which is apparently a dialogue between a new-born infant and its mother. The absence of quotation marks here may suggest the harmony between parent and baby, a bond of joy in which two identities are unified. But the child's point of view is implicitly subsumed by the mother, the only speaker in the second stanza – which may remind us that the child is subject to the parent's defining view.[3] There are other intimations of constraint here. In the design, the drooping bud at the right may recall the temporal process in which flowers unfold and decay, while in the song joy is at once a present state of being and a hope for the uncertain future.

The text, almost enclosed by curving brown flower stems, has been partly retouched with gold (the first line, and some words in the second stanza). There is gold in the title, in the mother's hair and collar, on the top curve of the right-hand stem, on the bud's top sepal, and along the right-hand edge of the plate. The border is formed at the top of fine green leaves or vines which curl gracefully over each corner. Vines continue down each side, curving and intertwining. Along the base fine black roots are sketched.

[1] See Bindman, *Blake as an Artist*, p. 60.

[2] Irene Chayes suggests that 'Infant Joy is an analogue of Cupid, Eros, the love god', and that the winged figure is a Psyche-figure 'waiting to receive Joy from the arms of the mother': Irene H. Chayes, 'The Presence of Cupid and Psyche', *Visionary Forms Dramatic*, edited by David V. Erdman and John E. Grant (Princeton, 1970), pp. 214–43 (p. 233).

[3] Lindsay notes: 'One of Blake's most characteristic devices in *Songs of Innocence* is the presentation of a monologue that subsumes a dialogue': *Blake: Songs of Innocence and Experience*, p. 19. The act of naming often assumes a special significance in Blake's work: it allows error to be defined and cast off (see *The Book of Urizen*, plate 12), but it is also associated with the fall into error. For a full discussion of this issue see Robert N. Essick, *William Blake and the Language of Adam* (Oxford, 1989), pp. 6–27.

Plate 26: A Dream

Once a dream did weave a shade,
O'er my Angel-guarded bed.
That an Emmet lost it's way
Where on grass methought I lay.

Troubled wilderd and forlorn
Dark benighted travel-worn,
Over many a tangled spray,
All heart-broke I heard her say.

O my children! do they cry,
Do they hear their father sigh.
Now they look abroad to see,
Now return and weep for me.

Pitying I drop'd a tear;
But I saw a glow-worm near:
Who replied. What wailing wight
Calls the watchman of the night.

I am set to light the ground,
While the beetle goes his round:
Follow now the beetles hum,
Little wanderer hie thee home.

The song draws on a number of ideas and motifs that would have been familiar to contemporary readers. John Adlard points out that the dor-beetle, which flies after sunset with a humming sound, was known as 'the watchman'.[1] The angel-guarded bed is an image that recurs in eighteenth-century hymns (see plates 20–21), while animal and insect fables were often used in hymns for children. Pinto compares Blake's poem to Bunyan's 'Upon the Pismire', and to Watts's 'The Ant', in both of which the ant is an examplar of industry and a reproach to idleness (as in Proverbs 6. 6–8). He notes that in Blake the 'moralizing has entirely disappeared'.[2] As in some other Innocence poems, the emphasis falls on distress and comfort. The pattern of losing and finding here recalls the 'Little Boy' poems (plates 13–14), but the dream structure complicates the pattern. The dreamer who reposes in the belief that his bed is 'Angel-guarded' finds his own faith (and presumably the fears that are comforted by that faith) reflected in his dream. There is a potential irony in this close association between dreaming and faith. The dream includes an image of the dreamer's own passivity ('on grass methought I lay'), and is seen to 'weave a shade' – offering comfort, perhaps, by protecting the dreamer from the harsh light of unpleasant truths. In copies B, C and D of the *Songs*, this song appears in Experience (see Introduction).

The lettering of the text is large (compare plates 22–23), leaving room only for marginal decoration. The blue wash over the plate is muted, creating a watery, dream-like effect. Some of the decorative foliage has been reinforced in black, but only the white figure of the watchman (at bottom right) is distinct, as he stands with a staff and lantern before the blue-black silhouette of a miniature tree or shrub. Above him to the left is a flying beetle. Another flies beside line 4. In some copies glow-worms and an emmet are seen, but they are not distinguishable here.[3] Several living forms appear around the title: a figure reclines on the first stroke of the 'A' (a dreamer?), another sitting in the 'D' has something in his lap; an angel flies on tiny wings below the 'e'. The bird soaring over 'dream' in the first line is perhaps an eagle, sometimes associated with vision in Blake's works.[4] The right margin has several tangled sprays, and the stanzas are divided by a variety of curving stems or leaf forms. A creeper winds down the left margin. The title, and the foliage above it, are reinforced with gold; there are faint traces of gold in the leaves to the right of stanzas 1 and 2, and in the spray by line 13. The border is a pair of curtains (out-lined in grey brown), hanging in folds either side, the tassled draw strings visible bottom left and right. At the bottom a grey vine sprouts a single leaf.

[1] Adlard also notes that the glow-worm was said (in a folksong) to light people 'home to bed' on moonless nights: John Adlard, *The Sports of Cruelty* (London, 1972), pp. 48–9.

[2] 'William Blake, Isaac Watts, and Mrs Barbauld', p. 77.

[3] Erdman notes that in some copies glow-worms are visible in a blade of grass after 'forlorn' in line 5, or after 'tear' in line 13, and after 'weep for me' in line 12: *IB* 67.

[4] See *The Marriage of Heaven and Hell* Plate 15 'In the third chamber was an Eagle with wings and feathers of air, he caused the inside of the cave to be infinite' (*E* 40; *K* 154).

Plate 27: On Anothers Sorrow

Can I see anothers woe,
And not be in sorrow too.
Can I see anothers grief,
And not seek for kind relief.

Can I see a falling tear.
And not feel my sorrows share,
Can a father see his child,
Weep, nor be with sorrow fill'd.

Can a mother sit and hear.
An infant groan an infant fear—
No no never can it be,
Never never can it be.

And can he who smiles on all
Hear the wren with sorrows small.
Hear the small birds grief & care
Hear the woes that infants bear—

And not sit beside the nest
Pouring pity in their breast.
And not sit the cradle near
Weeping tear on infants tear.

And not sit both night & day.
Wiping all our tears away.
O! no never can it be.
Never never can it be.

He doth give his joy to all,
He becomes an infant small,
He becomes a man of woe
He doth feel the sorrow too.

Think not. thou canst sigh a sigh,
And thy maker is not by.
Think not, thou canst weep a tear,
And thy maker is not near.

O! he gives to us his joy.
That our grief he may destroy
Till our grief is fled & gone
He doth sit by us and moan

This song echoes many of the preceding poems, and elaborates some of the central themes of Innocence. The divine mercy described here is like that promised in the Bible, which extends to all creatures (Matthew 10.29), wipes away human tears (Revelation 7.17), bears our griefs (Isaiah 53.3–4), and turns our sorrow to joy (John 16.20). As in 'The Divine Image' and other poems of Innocence, the divine and the human become identified. Working outwards from personal feeling to the protective instinct of parents, and then to the feelings of the 'maker' who 'becomes an infant small', the rhetorical questions suggest that empathy is an essential attribute of both humanity and divinity. Unlike the previous poem, or 'The Little Boy found', this vision involves no active intervention in human affairs. The maker does not prevent grief, or remove its cause. Although he is said to give us joy 'That our grief he may destroy', the last two lines imply simply that distress is lightened by the knowledge that it is shared. The comforter of this poem then, gives strength to endure, and promotes the human kindness that seeks to relieve distress in others.

The text leaves room only for marginal decorations, but visually the plate is dominated by the slender tree and encircling vine at the right, which display and mingle foliage, tendrils and green grapes in vigorous abundance. Several 'small birds' are visible: three (all touched with gold) are seen sitting on a branch beside line 4; others fly upwards (one by line 11, another beside line 5, a third, golden, by line 11). A large blue bird of paradise soars up beside the sixth and seventh stanzas (over 'He doth give his joy to all'). In the left margin the sky darkens in places, suggesting nightfall. Here among tendrils and a tangle of fine, vine-like branches several human forms appear. At the top a robed figure raises an arm as if to pray or to bless; below him the barely visible silhouette of a kneeling figure who raises both hands heavenwards by lines 7–9; beside stanza 7 the vague silhouette of a climber can be seen; and at the bottom, against a peaceful blue background, stands a golden-robed angel who resembles the watchman of the previous plate (in some copies he plays a pipe, not visible here).[1] The design recalls both the joyful daylight visions of some other Innocence plates (e.g. 5, 7, 8) and the angel-guarded night of others (e.g. 16, 20–21, 26). The title, and the scrolls that flourish from its capitals, are reinforced with gold, and there is gold among the vine-like forms in the left margin. The border is composed of green trellises, which form gothic and ogee arches, recalling those of the Combined Title-page and the Innocence frontispiece; vine tendrils curl over the top corners.

In its present position the plate forms a fitting conclusion to the series, as its text and design encompass several of the central themes and motifs of Innocence. The song reveals not only the emotional appeal of this state of the soul, but also the limitations. The speaker's vision of comfort is presented in terms that seem to exclude the possibility of parental indifference, of callous disregard for suffering, or indeed of a world in which children might be sold as chimney sweeps or slaves. The woes remain undefined, seen only in relation to the sympathy they should elicit. The vision seems to leave no room for moral outrage. For this we have to leave the state of Innocence, and enter the turbulent state of Experience.

[1] See *IB*, p. 68. Erdman also identifies a 'face of sorrow', the image of 'thy maker', beside lines 10–14, which I do not find here.

Plate 28: Frontispiece to *Songs of Experience*

In contrast to the cool shades of the Innocence frontispiece, the colouring here is rich and glowing. The warmth of the sky has been heightened at the left with fine gold shading. The shepherd has changed his blue costume for one of red. It has gold highlights, and there is gold on his chest. Advancing with right foot forward (not the left foot, as before), he no longer holds a pipe, but carries the winged child upon his head. The pose echoes representations of St. Christopher carrying the young Christ.[1] The child's hair, wings and body have gold highlights; the sky brightens behind him. The peaceful, open landscape here recalls those of plates 5 and 22, but the impression of warmth and plenty is modified by less reassuring features. A dark blue hill stands out starkly in the distance. Before it shadows gather on a rolling green plain where a single tree grows. The tree to the right forms an uncompromising straight line, like a grey metallic blade, in contrast to the gently curving and twining trees of the Innocence frontispiece. Black ivy leaves stand out against its bark.[2] The brows of both child and shepherd are slightly knit, their expressions are enigmatic. Both figures look out as if to fix attention of the reader. In the 'Introduction' to Innocence, the child controlled the piper with his demands, and then vanished. Here the shepherd seems more in control. The composition prepares us for the urgency of the Experience poems, which are introduced by the voice of a bard.

The upper half of the border is composed of (at the top) green and grey inter-woven vines, which form a diamond-shaped trellis with hanging tendrils at either side. In the lower half the vines form a straight trellis along the sides, and more diamond shapes along the bottom.

[1] Mitchell notes: 'Blake and his readers could have seen [such representations] in many English churches and in the works of European masters such as Dürer': W. J. T. Mitchell, *Blake's Composite Art* (Princeton, 1978), p. 6.

[2] The ivy is a traditional emblem of selfishness (see Baine, *The Scattered Portions*, p. 158).

Plate 29: Title-page for *Songs of Experience*

SONGS

of

EXPERIENCE

1794

The Author & Printer W Blake

This plate is both lighter and cooler than the Frontispiece. In reading the title the eye moves through vigorous life forms down to bare lettering reminiscent of a tombstone inscription. The word 'SONGS' here is more regular and restrained than on the Innocence title-page, but supports vegetation of comparable vigour: leaves, blue flowers, a coiling tendril. A tiny robed figure reaches up on a streamer from the first 'S', recalling the supplicants of Innocence (see plate 27). The word 'of' sprouts a vine with spiky leaves (perhaps ivy). To the left a girl in a flowing white dress reaches out towards a boy at right in a white body-tight costume: their postures suggest a joyful dance or an ecstatic greeting. 'EXPERIENCE' forms a bar across the page, separating the dynamic images above from the static scene below. The lettering of title (except 'of') has been reinforced with gold.

The lower part of the design apparently shows a brother and sister mourning the death of their mother and father, whose bodies are stretched out like monumental sculptures. The rectilinear symmetry of the composition presents a vivid contrast to the flowing curves of Innocence. Behind the figures a panelled wall appears, like a solid gate closed between pillars. The date '1794' is printed on the right pillar (the last numeral barely visible). In the foreground, beneath the blue-grey drapery of the bed or bier, a dull green mottled surface could be a carpet, or a stream.

The plate as whole appears to present an interior scene in an outdoor setting: the horizon is sealed to the mourners below, but their enclosed space opens into a larger and freer world above. In some copies the son and daughter are dressed in the same colours as the dancing boy and girl above, suggesting an identity (see *IB* 71–72). In other copies the dancers are naked. Here the colour scheme associates the white-robed bodies of the parents with the dancers: a reminder, perhaps, that the death of the body does not destroy individual identity.

The lettering at the foot of the page is in a gold panel, below which are signs of green and yellow vegetation. There is gold on the father's beard and pillow, and on the panelled wall – above the heads of the parents, around the mourners, and along the top edge. The border is a dull pink drapery, which descends from a knot or fold at the top.

Plate 30: Introduction.

Hear the voice of the Bard!
Who Present, Past, & Future sees
Whose ears have heard,
The Holy Word,
That walk'd among the ancient trees.

Calling the lapsed Soul
And weeping in the evening dew;
That might controll.
The starry pole;
And fallen fallen light renew!

O Earth O Earth return!
Arise from out the dewy grass;
Night is worn,
And the morn
Rises from the slumberous mass.

Turn away no more:
Why wilt thou turn away
The starry floor
The watry shore
Is givn thee till the break of day.

Unlike the piper of the 'Introduction' to Innocence, the Bard demands to be heard and speaks with authority. The fugitive child who inspires 'a song about a Lamb' is replaced by 'The Holy Word / That walk'd among the ancient trees'. The Bard has a sense of history, and a vision of human destiny.[1] The identification of 'the lapsed Soul' and 'Earth' gives another indication of the altered perspective of Experience. The Bard does not speak of a personal saviour who offers comfort to the distressed, but of a God who insists that the individual soul and the natural world are fallen, and who demands a universal resurrection. Nature is evoked here not in the sensuous terms of pastoral, but in more abstract terms that point to the existence of a predictable order which appears to govern life (the phrase 'starry pole' connects the rotation of the earth with the fixed order of the stars, while in the last stanza, the combination of 'starry floor' and 'watry shore' may give, in Frye's words, 'the sense of a created world as a protection against chaos').[2] In this view, creation is 'givn' as an act of mercy, and forms a limit to the fall. Life in nature is seen as a repose in darkness. If this vision seems grim in comparison with the instinctual, joyful vision of nature in Innocence, it entails a new sense of human potential: the conviction that humanity might wake in the sunrise of a new life and take 'controll' of its own destiny.

While the Bard's vision of the future may seem inspiring, his words may also seem confusing or confused. As several critics have noted, the ambiguous syntax and the absence of quotation marks tend to dissolve the distinctions between the Bard, the 'Holy Word', and the 'lapsed Soul'.[3] (Which of these 'might controll / The starry pole'?) The ambiguities suggest that the Bard is involved in the error he attempts to define. The reference to Genesis 3.8 in line 4 associates the Holy Word with the judging creator, who expelled humanity from Eden.[4] In contrast to the comforting saviour of Innocence, the Word seems remote from the world he wishes to save, set apart in his own grief. The commanding tone of the first stanza gives way to a more plaintive tone in stanzas three and four. The conviction that the soul is 'lapsed' involves judgement and reproach, which may confirm rather than remove the sense of distance between the human and the divine.

The design presents an image of chilly isolation. It shows the lapsed Soul or Earth reclining under a towering pillar of cloud, and looking out into the expanse of night. Her long hair is blown to the right, behind her face. Several white stars shine in the dark blue of the sky, the larger ones mostly five-pointed. The impression of coldness is relieved by traces of yellow and rose in the clouds (which could be the first signs of day-break), by Earth's yellow couch, by the pink of her naked body, and by the sun-like halo behind her, which suggests her divine potential. Several of the texts in Experience appear within clouds, as this one does – a device which seems to indicate the speaker's confusion. Gold is used in the title, in the shading on Earth's couch, and in fine rays from her halo. The border is a simple rectangular frame of green and brown. Brown tendrils curl around the top corners. There is some smudging inside the border, right of the title.

---

[1] The appeal to Earth in stanza three echoes Deuteronomy 31.1, Jeremiah 22.29, and Isaiah 60.1. The Bard is implicitly aligned with the 'ancient' tradition of biblical prophecy.

[2] Northrop Frye, 'Blake's Introduction to Experience', *Blake: A Collection of Critical Essays* (Englewood Cliffs, New Jersey, 1966), p. 28.

[3] See for example, F. R. Leavis, *Revaluation* (London, 1936), pp. 140–2; Stanley Gardner, *Infinity on the Anvil* (Oxford, 1954), pp. 118–19.

[4] Genesis 3.8 'And they heard the voice of the Lord God walking in the garden in the cool of the day: and Adam and his wife hid themselves from the presence of the Lord God amongst the trees of the garden.'

Plate 31: Earth's Answer

Earth raisd up her head.
From the darkness dread & drear.
Her light fled:
Stony dread!
And her locks cover'd with grey despair.

Prison'd on watry shore
Starry Jealousy does keep my den
Cold and hoar
Weeping o'er
I hear the father of the ancient men

Selfish father of men
Cruel jealous selfish fear
Can delight
Chain'd in night
The virgins of youth and morning bear.

Does spring hide its joy
When buds and blossoms grow?
Does the sower?
Sow by night?
Or the plowman in darkness plow?

Break this heavy chain.
That does freeze my bones around
Selfish! vain!
Eternal bane!
That free Love with bondage bound.

In this song the Bard's view of existence, given in the 'Introduction', is both challenged and partially confirmed. The challenge is direct: from Earth's point of view, creation does not seem a merciful limit to the fall, but a prison; the traditional image of the creator who demands obedience ('Starry Jealousy') seems profoundly unnatural, as it promotes repression and thus inhibits the regeneration that the Bard foresees.[1] But Earth's passionate protest implicitly confirms the Bard's view – in that she sees her own condition as limited, and assumes that the limits are imposed (or, as the Bard says, 'givn'). Her view, like his, seems governed by the Holy Word ('I hear the father of the ancient men'), and the reproachful voices in both poems suggest a consciousness frozen into helpless inactivity.

Nevertheless, there is hope in Earth's yearning for delight and sunrise, a hope that seems answered in the accompanying design. Compared with the previous plate, this one is sunny and warm. A vine springs from 'Stony dread' and sprouts leaves in the right-hand margin and above the title, before descending left of the text (where it is streaked with gold). Another growing from 'father of' has tendrils, leaves and purple and pink grapes (a reminder that spring does not hide its joy). It is touched with gold as it flourishes between the lines of stanza 2. The flame-like leaves that snake down beside the last three stanzas are met at bottom right by a serpent of blue and russet, with eye, tongue and jaw of gold, and golden highlights on its body. More gold shines around the serpent's head and body (at right). This reminder of the Genesis myth relates Earth to Eve, whose desire was punished as sinful. Here the serpent seems glorified, as if in vindication of desire.[2]

There is gold in the title. The border is a simple rectangular frame (green at bottom, grey elsewhere, reinforced by gold at top and left). At top left and right corners, rams' heads break into the plate, the faces and horns highlighted with gold. Brief pink scrolls stream out at either side – part of a festal decking. The heads recall those in Blake's Job series (plates 1 and 21), which are associated with the sacrifice of the spirit to the letter.[3] Here they refer to the sacrifice of joy and delight to 'selfish fear'.

[1] For the biblical sources of Blake's phrase 'Starry jealousy' see, for example, Genesis 1.16; Exodus 20.5; 34.14; Deuteronomy 4.24.

[2] Wicksteed notes that the poem was originally written in answer to two little notebook poems claiming liberty for love. *Blake's Innocence and Experience*, p. 147.

[3] David Bindman, *The Complete Graphic Works of William Blake*, nos. 626, 646.

Plate 32: The Clod & the Pebble

Love seeketh not Itself to please.
Nor for itself hath any care;
But for another gives its ease.
And builds a Heaven in Hells despair.

So sung a little Clod of Clay,
Trodden with the cattles feet;
But a Pebble of the brook.
Warbled out these metres meet.

Love seeketh only Self to please,
To bind another to Its delight;
Joys in anothers loss of ease.
And builds a Hell in Heavens despite.

The Clod of Clay's view that love 'for another gives its ease' may recall the innocence of 'On Another's Sorrow' (plate 27). But as the Clod makes no mention of the self-delighting aspect of love, or the pleasure of giving, its claims may suggest a self-denying attitude that can lead to repression and self-righteousness. The Pebble's claim that love 'Joys in anothers loss of ease' may refer not only to a malevolent delight in the emotional conquest of others, but also to the predatory aspect of pity, which feeds on its object. The phrase 'Heavens despite' is characteristically ambiguous: it expresses the selfish defiance of the Pebble, but also hints at the hypocrisy of the Clod of Clay. Frosch notes that the 'debate could never take place in Innocence, where children conceive of themselves as connected with otherness. Once they are aware of themselves as separate and thus have to wonder whether to please themselves or the other, they are out of Innocence'.[1] Both voices generalize about love; in doing so they transform one aspect of love into an absolute, and attempt to negate its contrary aspect.

The sunny illustrations that accompany the text seem remote in mood from the problematic voices of the song. In the upper part of the plate, beneath a blue and pink sky, four sheep (one a ram) and two light-brown oxen drink at a 'brook'. The sheep at the left is clearly standing in the water: no doubt these animals tread the clay as they drink, and their feet may be vulnerable to the pebble. The backs of the oxen appear to be in shade, although the overhanging branch from the tree at the right is leafless. The fleeces have abundant gold shading. More sheep appear behind those who drink. In the distance, behind a strip of green, the dark blue of the sea can be seen.

The text area, washed with yellow and pink, forms a warm sky for the scene below. A duck with red and green wings, and a fine speckling of red, blue and purple on its neck and breast, swims in a blue river. On the grassy bank in the foreground two frogs appear either side of a worm. A vine sprouts and forks near the worm, curving up the right-hand margin and putting out leaves there. The drinking, swimming and leaping in this sunny design would seem to express instinctual drives and satisfactions rather than self-conscious 'Love'.[2]

In the title, 'CLOD', '&' with its the banner-like streamer, and 'PEBBLE' have been reinforced with gold. The sides of the border are composed of long green shepherd's crooks (perhaps a reminder of what is missing in the song: the self-delighting and protective love of the Shepherd; see plate 5). A few reeds grow at the bottom, and vines snake upward beside the text (the vine at the left curves into the plate to greet the vines that sprout near the beginning of the title). Along the base patches of green suggest water.

---

[1] Thomas R. Frosch, 'The Borderline of Innocence and Experience', *Approaches to Teaching Blake's*

'*Songs of Innocence and of Experience*', edited by Robert F. Gleckner and Mark L. Greenberg (New York, 1989), pp. 74–9 (p. 77).

[2] Wicksteed suggests that the design shows the interdependence of organic life: 'The duck preys upon the frogs, the frogs upon the still lower life, all finally dependent on the worm and the earth', *Blake's Innocence and Experience*, p. 173. But the design appears to show a moment of peaceful co-existence. Jean Hagstrum associates the appearance of the cattle with fallen nature and 'an oppressive society that calls for passive humility and obedience': 'William Blake's "The Clod and the Pebble" ', *Restoration and Eighteenth-Century Literature: Essays in Honour of Alan Dugald McKillop*, edited by Carroll Camden (Chicago, 1963), pp. 381–8 (p. 386).

Plate 33: Holy Thursday

Is this a holy thing to see.
In a rich and fruitful land.
Babes reducd to misery.
Fed with cold and usurous hand?

Is that trembling cry a song?
Can it be a song of joy?
And so many children poor?
It is a land of poverty!

And their sun does never shine.
And their fields are bleak & bare.
And their ways are fill'd with thorns
It is eternal winter there.

For where-e'er the sun does shine.
And where-e'er the rain does fall:
Babe can never hunger there,
Nor poverty the mind appall.

In this companion piece to the 'Holy Thursday' of Innocence (plate 19), there is no attempt to describe the annual thanksgiving service for charity school children, or to suggest its emotional appeal. Instead the speaker looks more generally at the 'rich and fruitful land' that has 'so many children poor'. From this point of view, poverty seems unnatural, created by and for a social system based on profit, not pity: children are 'reducd' to misery and then 'Fed with cold and usurous hand'. The view encompasses not only the cruelty and exploitation practiced in charity schools, but the wider moral confusion of a land that fails to acknowledge the gulf between its practice and its preaching.[1] In the final stanza the 'eternal winter' endured by the poor is implicitly contrasted with the comfort that will prevail when Christ dwells among those that serve Him (Revelation 7.16 'They shall hunger no more').

The insistent rhythms of the song help to create a powerful sense of moral outrage. But when viewed in the light of the Innocence poem, this speaker's description of the children's song as 'a trembling cry' may suggest an unwillingness to acknowledge the presence of vitality or joy in the victims of poverty. In this respect the judgement seems to involve a retreat into generalization, and an emotional hardening, that offers little prospect of escape from the human coldness it condemns.[2]

In the scene above the text, the angular landscape seems bleak and wintry. The blue of the sky, streaked with light clouds, darkens to the right behind craggy white mountains. On the grass before a light strip of water an infant lies stiff and white, as if dead or dying. The woman stands at a distance, like a shocked passer-by, hands splayed out in a gesture of dismay. Her gown and groomed hair do not suggest poverty, and the stiffness of her pose betrays no inclination to embrace or examine the child. She seems about to walk on (her left foot is forward). Presumably the scene illustrates the coexistence of poverty and riches in the same land. The tree at the right sends out a leafless branch over woman and child, forming a partial frame, but giving no shelter. The grey tones of the bark give it a rock-like appearance.

In the right margin, huge and luxuriantly green oak leaves lie in clusters or singly, on which more victims of poverty appear. By one leaf a boy in blue stands, head in hands, near a woman in pink who kneels in an attitude of despair. A naked child clings around the woman's neck, excluded rather than embraced by her arm. Above this group the sky darkens. In the bottom right corner, a naked figure lies supine on fallen leaves, arms spread. Gardner relates this image to Hogarth's design, *The Foundlings* (used on the Subscription Roll of the Foundling Hospital), which shows a 'dropped' (or abandoned) child lying naked and exposed by a roadside near the Hospital's door.[3] In this context the leaves may recall the association of the oak with Druid sacrifice.

A vine grows up the left margin by the first three stanzas, and sprouts lily-shaped leaves under the title. Elsewhere in Experience (plate 43) the lily is associated with unselfish love. Its presence here emphasizes what is lacking in 'a land of poverty'. There is gold in the title, on the vine at the left of stanza 1, and behind the dark spikes of vegetation at bottom right. The barren branches and spiky leaves in the border reflect the vision of 'eternal winter' in the song.

[1] For a full account of the charity school movement, and of the harsh conditions experienced in some schools, see M. G. Jones, *The Charity School Movement* (Cambridge, 1938).

[2] Glen suggests that the poem dramatizes 'that "poverty" of spirit which, cutting itself off in angry disenchantment from that which is before it, is finally reduced to dismayed passivity in the face of a world which is seen as unalterably given', *Vision and Disenchantment*, p. 123.

[3] Stanley Gardner, *'Innocence' and 'Experience' Retraced*, pp. 121–3.

Plates 34–35: The Little Girl Lost

In futurity
I prophetic see.
That the earth from sleep.
(Grave the sentence deep)

Shall arise and seek
For her maker meek:
And the desert wild
Become a garden mild.

In the southern clime,
Where the summers prime.
Never fades away;
Lovely Lyca lay.

Seven summers old
Lovely Lyca told,
She had wanderd long.
Hearing wild birds song.

Sweet sleep come to me
Underneath this tree;
Do father, mother weep.—
"Where can Lyca sleep".

Lost in desart wild
Is your little child.
How can Lyca sleep.
If her mother weep.

If her heart does ake.
Then let Lyca wake;
If my mother sleep,
Lyca shall not weep.

Frowning frowning night,
O'er this desart bright.
Let thy moon arise.
While I close my eyes.

Sleeping Lyca lay:
While the beasts of prey,
Come from caverns deep,
View'd the maid asleep

The kingly lion stood
And the virgin view'd,
Then he gambold round
O'er the hallowd ground:

Leopards, tygers play,
Round her as she lay;
While the lion old,
Bow'd his mane of gold,

And her bosom lick,
And upon her neck,
From his eyes of flame,
Ruby tears there came;

While the lioness,
Loos'd her slender dress,
And naked they convey'd
To caves the sleeping maid.

Plates 35–36: The Little Girl Found

All the night in woe,
Lyca's parents go:
Over vallies deep.
While the desarts weep.

Tired and woe-begone.
Hoarse with making moan:
Arm in arm seven days.
They trac'd the desart ways.

Seven nights they sleep.
Among shadows deep:
And dream they see their child
Starv'd in desert wild.

Pale thro' pathless ways
The fancied image strays.
Famish'd, weeping, weak
With hollow piteous shriek

Rising from unrest,
The trembling woman prest,
With feet of weary woe;
She could no further go.

In his arms he bore.
Her arm'd with sorrow sore:
Till before their way,
A couching lion lay.

Turning back was vain,
Soon his heavy mane.
Bore them to the ground;
Then he stalk'd around.

Smelling to his prey,
But their fears allay.
When he licks their hands:
And silent by them stands.

They look upon his eyes
Fill'd with deep surprise:
And wondering behold.
A spirit arm'd in gold.

On his head a crown
On his shoulders down,
Flow'd his golden hair.
Gone was all their care.

Follow me he said,
Weep not for the maid;
In my palace deep.
Lyca lies asleep.

Then they followed,
Where the vision led;
And saw their sleeping child,
Among tygers wild.

To this day they dwell
In a lonely dell
Nor fear the wolvish howl,
Nor the lions growl.

These two songs, etched as a unified sequence, originally appeared in the Innocence series.[1] In its present context the first song recalls the 'Introduction' to Experience. The prophetic voice of the first two stanzas (like the voice of the 'Bard') heralds the resurrection of the sleeping earth in an indefinite 'futurity'. This opening encourages us to see a relationship between the sleep of 'earth' and the sleep of Lyca in the tale that follows. At first sight the story seems to have the simplicity of a traditional folktale; but as often in Blake, the simplicity is deceptive.[2]

In some respects the two songs seem to be counterparts of 'The Little Boy lost' and 'The Little Boy found' in Innocence. In contrast to the Little Boy's sense of abandonment and distress, and his anxiety to follow his 'Father', Lyca thinks primarily of her parents' anxiety, and is prepared to sleep in the 'desart wild' after her wandering. Unlike the Boy, she seems to have a belief in her own safety, which may recall the faith of the speaker in 'Night'. The tradition that the lion will not harm a virgin is evoked here to suggest the invulnerability of innocence in a world of savage predatory appetites. The lion that licks her recalls both the protective beast of plate 21 and the innocence of plate 23. But if the lion and lioness protect Lyca, and make her 'slender dress' seem unnecessary, they also take possession of her.

While the first part of the sequence focuses on Lyca, the second is more concerned with her parents. Whereas Lyca slips unconsciously into the care of wild beasts, the parents must first pass through fear.[3] For them the night is a source of terrifying dreams, and the 'unrest' they endure seems typical of Experience. The mother becomes 'arm'd with sorrow', as if protecting herself from the greater anxiety of hope and disappointment (her condition is comparable to that of the speaker on plate 41). But as in 'The Little Boy found', distress is a condition in which comfort appears. What initially seem to be hungry predators are found to be the providential protectors of their daughter. The parents' triumph over fear thus recalls the sustaining faith of Innocence, although there is no mention of Lyca awakening, and no return from the 'lonely dell'.

The sequence explores Innocence from the point of view of the prophet or bard; and since the prophet looks for a universal resurrection (the return of earth to her maker), in his account the faith of Innocence seems ultimately inadequate. The final situation recalls the biblical image of faith as a triumph over the threatening power of the lion (see Daniel 6, and Hebrews 11.33), an image used by Charles Wesley in his hymn 'Meet and right it is to praise':

> Here, as in the lion's den,
> Undevoured we still remain[4]

The prophetic speaker of Blake's song shows that this kind of triumph over fear reconciles individuals to their fallen condition, rather that liberating them from it. From this point of view, the comforter imprisons. Indeed, the protecting spirit in this song seems to use fear as an instrument to draw his 'prey' into his power:

> Soon his heavy mane
> Bore them to the ground
> Then he stalk'd around
> Smelling to his prey

The identification of the lion and the saviour here takes on a quite different significance from that in plate 21. If the spirit with a crown and flowing golden hair suggests a Christ-like being, he is not a shepherd but a king who dwells in a palace. The imagery carries with it suggestions of hierarchy, military power, an existence organized for self-protection: the spirit is 'arm'd' in gold, just as the mother was 'arm'd' with sorrow. Compared with the shepherd, this image of providence seems easier to reconcile with the machinery of state power. The parents' experience is thus quite unlike that of their daughter, who entered the lion's realm naked and unconscious. They are protected by a spirit that seems at once to allay and to reflect their fears. Although they are reunited with Lyca, all remain in a dwelling that seems remote from the world at large.

[179]

If the bard's story tends to expose the inadequacy of Innocence – both the instinctual ('naked') innocence of Lyca, and the organized innocence of her parents – the introductory stanzas show that his own ideal is 'a garden mild'. In this copy of the *Songs* there is no mention of gardens in Innocence, the realm of pastoral fields and village greens. Gardens are more characteristic of Experience, and are usually associated with temptation and withdrawal into private pleasures. Thus the bard foresees a transformation which itself seems limited, and which may offer no real alternative to the 'lonely dell' where Lyca sleeps. As in the 'Introduction', the prophetic vision seems bound by the horizons of Experience. As we might expect, the ambiguities of the tale are reflected in the accompanying illustrations.

The scene on the first plate is apparently the 'garden mild' in which earth and maker are united in a loving embrace. The lines of the design are flowing and graceful. Behind the lovers rise delicate curving willow branches and meandering vines. In the left margin a vine, gold at the top, forms a wave-like pattern. Tiny leaves and two bells appear on its offshoots (two more bells by stanza 3 are partially overpainted). On the lowest offshoot sits a brown and pink bird of paradise, while another flies down towards it. A serpent of gold and blue coils and twists on a branch between the second and third stanza, looking away from the couple below; it stands out sharply against the lightest area of the plate. The presence of the serpent recalls the myth of Eden, and may remind us that the garden was lost because our first parents were not content to remain within its limits. The delicate trees offer neither shade nor fruit, and may even seem undeveloped. The female is not wholly absorbed in her lover – her body is turned away from him, and she points upwards, as if in aspiration, towards a blue bird of paradise that flies up beneath the title. She recalls Milton's Eve, whose fall began when she insisted on withdrawing from Adam (and who dreamed of flying up to the clouds, *Paradise Lost* V, 86–90). The 'garden mild' may constitute an ideal for the bard, but its adequacy here seems questionable. There are hints of darkness gathering at top right and bottom left.

The colouring of the diaphanous robes harmonize easily with the blue, pink and yellow of the background. Gold shines in the spaces between the figures, by her breast and his back, and around the green leaf at her foot. More gold appears in the title (except 'he', and the 'i' of 'Little') and in the sweeping line above it; along the left side of the frame; in flecks on the willow trunk, and in highlights in its hanging fronds and on the vine that grows around it. In the border, opposite stanzas 3–8, orange and green vines display tiny leaves and bells. The left side echoes the rhythm of the vine in the left margin of the plate.

The second plate is finely finished. The figure in the red dress is presumably Lyca, shown as a young woman rather than as the seven-year-old child of the song. Her pose and open-mouthed expression indicate distress, but if she is 'Lost in desart wild' the luxuriantly green forest into which she gazes is neither dark nor threatening. The tree behind her is leafless, but it sends a branch out over her to form a protective arch with a branch from the tree at right. In the middle distance three more sturdy trees are grouped together, their leaves forming a broad canopy that recalls the protective oaks of plates 6 and 8. Behind Lyca's head fine blue and green speckles suggest dense vegetation.

In the lower portion, the jungle cat that stands as if sniffing the air has a wide eye and the hint of a smile. Its rich colouring of blue, red, brown and gold suggests both stripes and spots (it could be a tiger, a leopard or a lioness). The mottled grey tree that arches over beast and text is leafless.[5] In the left margin it meets a coiling and curving vine, which has tiny leaves and bells. The design here in some respects parallels that on the first plate: the left margin has the same motif; in the right margin the barren arching tree gives a distant echo of the willow's more graceful lines, while the beast takes the place of the lovers. As in the upper portion of this plate, the scene appears to hold the terrors of Experience in balance with the reassuring protection of Innocence.

The title is gold and there is gold in the vine opposite stanzas 1–3, in its upper three leaves, and on the grass beneath the trees. The vines in the border have three distinct rhythms at either side.

The text on the third plate appears in a narrow space between the massive entwined trees at the right, and the sapling with coiling vine at left. The composition gives the impression of a deep chasm, at the foot of which three naked children play with a lion and lioness. At bottom left a young golden-haired woman lies naked on the grass, presumably the sleeping Lyca without her 'slender dress'. The tree trunks are largely covered with green vegetation (flecked occasionally with gold), which gives the scene a leafy, pastoral appearance. The lion and lioness both have gold highlights in their eyes and on their bodies. There is gold in the sky around the two children at the left, on the sapling and vine above them, in their hair, and in the hair of the girl in the middle.

Here the powerful energies typical of Experience have been transformed, to create a protective environment that resembles – but is quite different from – the pastoral scenes of Innocence. The children at play here recall both the child in plate 23, who plays with a lamb, and the prophetic vision of Isaiah 11.6.[6] The 'desart wild' has become an earthly paradise which invites comparison with the Edenic vision of the first plate. There the human figures embrace beneath slender, delicate trees. Here massive trees embrace, dwarfing the human figures. There the woman points upwards; here the woman sleeps. As an image of paradise this scene seems no more adequate than the first scene, although it helps to clarify the bard's paradoxical vision of Innocence.

The border is composed of simple vines, green at the sides and top, blue black along the base.

[1] The sequence was transferred to Experience when the two series were combined (see Introduction).

[2] The complexities of the tale have been explored in a number of elaborate readings. See, for example, Kathleen Raine, *Blake and Tradition*, I, 128–9, and Irene H. Chayes, 'Little Girls Lost: Problems of a Romantic Archetype', in *Blake: A Collection of Essays*, edited by Northrop Frye.

[3] The seven days and nights of the parents' ordeal correspond to the seven ages of torment suffered by Nebuchadnezzar (Daniel 4.32).

[4] *A Collection of Hymns*, p. 230. Wesley's hymn amply demonstrates the use of fear to encourage commitment to the Saviour.

[5] In some copies the tree sprouts two blossoms in the left margin (see *IB* 35). In this copy the blossoms have been over-painted.

[6] 'The wolf shall also dwell with the lamb, and the leopard shall lie down with the kid; and the calf and the young lion and the fatling together; and a little child shall lead them'.

Plate 37: The Chimney Sweeper

A little black thing among the snow:
Crying weep, weep, in notes of woe!
Where are thy father & mother? say?
They are both gone up to the church to pray.

Because I was happy upon the heath.
And smil'd among the winters snow:
They clothed me in the clothes of death.
And taught me to sing the notes of woe.

And because I am happy. & dance & sing.
They think they have done me no injury:
And are gone to praise God & his Priest & King
Who make up a heaven of our misery.

In the Innocence version of 'The Chimney Sweeper' the child spoke without an introduction. In this Experience version the sweep is first seen from the point of view of a passer-by, who perceives only wretchedness, 'A little black thing'. The sweep's account of himself makes this 'woe' seem an outward appearance imposed by the parents. Even while he explains the cause of 'our misery' he says 'I am happy'. The insight of Experience does not preclude the joy of Innocence here (as it does in the 'Holy Thursday' song of Experience). To the child, joy seems natural ('I was happy upon the heath'), while the adults seem to 'make up' both the misery and the Heaven that justifies it. His vision not only reveals the perverse hypocrisy of a society that condones the exploitation of children, it casts a new light on a religious system that it is founded upon, and celebrates, the sacrifice of innocence.

The scene below the text places the child more clearly in his working environment. The presence of snow emphasizes his function as well as his misery: the cold weather makes fires and swept chimneys necessary; he works as an outcast to help others keep warm. Alone on a snow-covered street, he plods on past a closed door, a huge black sack on his back, looking up open-mouthed at a dark, comfortless sky. The dominant impression of coldness is relieved by the warmth of the print colour, and by the liberal use of gold, which highlights his features (including his eyes), his body and sack, the falling and fallen snow, the pebbles in the foreground and the front of the house at right.

The plate as a whole is lightened by the sky-blue and white of the text area. There is more gold here: in the title and the banners that stream down from some of its letters, in the flame-like form at the top right corner, along the bottom edge of the text panel at the left, down the left edge of the plate by stanza 1. The brown and yellow creeper that winds from the final 'r' turns gold as it curls around 'woe'. The border is formed of a blue snow cloud around the top half of the plate, and clinging snow around the lower half.

Plate 38: Nurses Song

When the voices of children. are heard on the green
And whisprings are in the dale:
The days of my youth rise fresh in my mind,
My face turns green and pale.

Then come home my children. the sun is gone down
And the dews of night arise
Your spring & your day. are wasted in play
And your winter and night in disguise.

The song is the counterpart of the 'Nurse's Song' in Innocence (plate 24): lines 1, 5 and 6 in each poem are identical. The nurse of Experience hears no 'laughing . . . on the hill'; the ambiguous 'whisprings . . . in the dale' have a revealing significance for her, as she remembers her own youth and shows symptoms of envy and frustration. In the light of these symptoms, her words in stanza two seem to project onto the children her own sense of 'wasted' life, of guilt, repressed desire and lost freedom. The transition from day to night here becomes associated with a withdrawal from childhood pleasures into the dark constraints of adulthood, which 'disguise' genuine feelings.

The scene below the text resembles one of the plates Blake engraved for the frontispiece of Mary Wollstonecraft's *Original Stories* (see Introduction). Standing on grass before an open doorway, the nurse attends carefully to a young boy's hair. The lines of her red dress are restrained, her face expresses satisfaction (both dress and face have gold highlights). The boy's pose, like his impassive face, suggests proud self-possession. His yellow suit is shaded with gold and his eyes and hair are golden. Behind him a girl in mauve sits in the doorway, perhaps reading. The discrepancy between the fretful voice in the poem, and the satisfied nurse in the picture, casts new light on the nurse's reference to 'disguise'. Her careful preparation of her golden young master may remind us that, compared with the simple freedoms of childhood, the adult world he will soon enter is formal and to that extent disguises human nature. The visual separation of the boy from the girl may point to the segregation of the sexes that occurs as children approach the threshold of adult life. In contrast to the impression of rigidity created by the standing figures and the lines of the doorway, the vines at either side are vigorous and abundant. Ironically, the red of the nurse's dress associates her visually with the grapes.

The title has been reinforced with gold: the first 'N' puts out a golden line that runs along the top edge of the plate, while a tiny figure reclines in a curving leaf on the first stroke of the letter; a golden lily sprouts from the 'S' of 'Song' (anticipating perhaps, the unguarded love associated with the 'Lilly' on plate 43, and which seems conspicuously absent here). In the second stanza a vine grows from 'arise'; it hangs a tendril, leaf and bunch of grapes down by the door, meanders up between the stanzas with more leaves and tendrils, and sends an offshoot up and around to the end of line 2. The border is composed of yellow vines either side, which each put out four branches towards the edge of the plate. Unlike the vines inside the plate area, these are largely bare; they curve smoothly over the upper corners and form gold branches and leaves at the top. There are black roots at the bottom.

Plate 39: The Sick Rose

O Rose thou art sick.
The invisible worm.
That flies in the night
In the howling storm:

Has found out thy bed
Of crimson joy:
And his dark secret love
Does thy life destroy.

In Blake's day the word 'sick' had several meanings: as well as 'ill' it could mean, for example, 'pale' or 'wan', but also 'corrupt through sin or wrong doing' (as in Charles Wesley's version of Psalm 6.1 'And heal my Soul diseas'd and sick'). The first line of this song can therefore be read as an expression of sympathy or as an accusation.[1] The imagery of physical corruption does not in itself imply guilt, but the sexual connotations of the speaker's terms might have this implication ('Has found out thy bed'). As a victim the rose seems at once innocent and implicated in her injury. The speaker's horror might suggest unselfish concern, or an attitude to love that is essentially fearful – an attitude that is perhaps a manifestation of the shame that leads to 'dark secret love'.[2]

The sick rose that droops around the text is a pale pink (compare the deep crimson of the blossom in 'Infant Joy', plate 25), although the edges of the petals are lined with gold, and some leaves (especially the serated edges) have gold highlights. From the heart of the rose a young woman emerges, with arms stretched out as if in terror; her mouth may be open, but her expression is indeterminate. Her body, hair and face shine with gold. She is the human form of the rose, its blighted life and joy. The worm that coils around her appears to pass through her heart. The thorns, picked out in black, create an enclosed space quite unlike the protective spaces of Innocence. At top left a caterpillar is poised to devour a leaf. On the stems below, two figures in golden robes appear in attitudes of despair or shame. One lies on the thorns, clutching its cowled head, left leg drawn up, foot hanging in air; the train of its robe curves down the stem, forming two curls. The other kneels with right hand raised to its hidden face, golden hair streaming down. Spiky leaves appear in the bottom right corner, and at the base of the rose stem; at the left edge of the plate another stem rises up, curling out of the frame and then returning to cross the top left corner. Spikes or serrations thus appear at each corner of the frame.

The title, and some words in the text, have been retouched in gold. The border has no foliage: its spare lines form arches and whips at the top.

1 Lindsay suggests that the song is 'a Blakean restatement of Adam's first speech to Eve after her fall [in *Paradise Lost*]', *Blake: Songs of Innocence and Experience*, p. 46.

2 Elizabeth Langland argues that the poem subverts 'traditional literary imagery to implicate readers themselves in the blighting and blasting process'. Elizabeth Langland, 'Blake's Feminist Revision of Literary Tradition in "The Sick Rose" ', *Critical Paths: Blake and the Argument of Method*, edited by Dan Miller, March Rracher and Donald Ault (London, 1987), pp. 225–43 (pp. 241–3). Michael Riffaterre argues that the meaning conveyed by the poem 'has nothing to do with love or sex. This meaning is the inseparability of Beauty and its Destruction, Death as the other face of Beauty', Michael Riffaterre, 'The Self-sufficient Text', *Essential Articles for the Study of William Blake, 1970–1984*, edited by Nelson Hilton (Hamden, Connecticut, 1986), pp. 57–74 (p. 72).

Plate 40: The Fly.

Little Fly
Thy summers play,
My thoughtless hand
Has brush'd away.

Am not I
A fly like thee?
Or art not thou
A man like me?

For I dance
And drink & sing;
Till some blind hand
Shall brush my wing.

If thought is life
And strength & breath;
And the want
Of thought is death;

Then am I
A happy fly,
If I live,
Or if I die.

The skipping rhythms in this poem, and the speaker's sense of identity with a fly, may recall the state of Innocence.[1] But the view of life that emerges here is quite unlike the providential view typical of that state. The visionary speakers of Innocence, such as the Little Black Boy (plates 9–10) or Tom Dacre (plate 12), seem to have no fear of death because they see it as the beginning of a new and more joyful existence. Their faith is sustained by the vision of a loving redeemer who will liberate them from the trials of mortal life. The speaker in 'The Fly' takes comfort in a contrary view. The intimations of joy in his song ('For I dance / And drink & sing') inspire no thoughts of a saviour.[2] He thinks instead of the 'blind hand' that will terminate his life. The self-defeating nature of his ambiguous logic suggests unconscious irony: if thought is life, then the 'thoughtless' speaker is already lifeless; if the want of thought is death, and one can be 'happy' in death, then happiness becomes equated with the want of thought. In either case death will indeed make little difference. His words might be taken to mean that death is an illusion because thought is indestructible, but this conclusion, like the possible alternatives, is not supported by the conviction that comforts the speakers in Innocence; it depends on the blind chance implicit in his use of 'If'.[3]

The scene of 'summers play' below the text may, like the song, recall the world of Innocence, but the barren trees and bare horizon relate the activities here to the grimmer world of Experience. Dark, mottled lines on the tree at the right suggest ivy. The young woman, dressed rather like the mother of plate 48, looks down intently and unsmilingly at the little boy she is helping to walk. His expression is bright but not playful. As John Grant notes, the young girl at the left who is about to strike a shuttlecock 'plays a game requiring *two* players by herself'.[4] The three figures may recall plate 38, where the boy receives attention while the girl sits alone. The age differences here also suggest a circular pattern – the girl who plays may in time become a mother, and supervise her own child. Like the poem the design points to the transience of life; unlike the designs of Innocence, it gives no hint of spiritual comfort within the cycle of nature. As on plate 30, the text appears within a cloud as if to indicate the speaker's confusion.[5] To the right of the last stanza is the silhouette of a shapeless bird or fly.

The plate is visually rich and glowing, like the Frontispiece of Experience. The yellow and pink of the cloud dominate the sky. The mother's purple dress and the diaphanous pink robes of the children add to the impression of summer warmth. Gold has been applied plentifully: some words in stanza 1 have been retouched with it; it shines in the sky above the boy's head, behind the battledore, and to the left of stanza 1. There are gold highlights on the clothing and hair of the figures, and on the grass at the woman's feet. The title and the filament-like branches around it are gold. In the border, green vines make three waves and seven loops at either side.

[1] In Hagstrum's reading, the poem seems very close indeed to the mood of Innocence. He argues that the poem shows 'a conversion . . . from thoughtless insensitivity', a conversion 'which in reality provides the conditions under which joy can be preserved'. Jean Hagstrum, 'The Fly', *William Blake: Essays for Samuel Foster Damon*, edited by Alvin H. Rosenfeld (Providence, 1969), pp. 368–82 (p. 380).

[2] The song echoes Cowley's poem 'The Grasshopper', which celebrates the happiness of the 'Voluptuous . . . and Epicurean animal', that will 'drink, and dance, and sing' until sated, and then retire to endless rest.

[3] The argument could be seen as a variant of 'Pascal's wager': 'if death is not the end of thought, then I'll be happy; if it is the end of thought, happily I'll know nothing of it'.

[4] John E. Grant, 'Interpreting Blake's "The Fly" ', in *Blake: A Collection of Critical Essays*, edited by Northrop Frye, pp. 32–55 (p. 47).

[5] See Grant, op. cit., p. 48.

Plate 41: The Angel

I Dreamt a Dream! what can it mean?
And that I was a maiden Queen:
Guarded by an Angel mild;
Witless woe, was neer beguil'd!

And I wept both night and day
And he wip'd my tears away
And I wept both day and night
And hid from him my hearts delight

So he took his wings and fled:
Then the morn blush'd rosy red:
I dried my tears & armd my fears,
With ten thousand shields and spears.

Soon my Angel came again;
I was arm'd, he came in vain:
For the time of youth was fled
And grey hairs were on my head

As we have seen, the 'Angel-guarded bed' is a familiar image in eighteenth-century hymns (see plates 16 and 28). This speaker's dream recalls the divine comfort envisaged in 'On Anothers Sorrow', where the maker sits 'both night & day / Wiping all our tears away'. The woes in that poem are unspecified, but here the 'Witless woe' is implicitly a symptom of repressed passion ('Witless' implies both lack of understanding and a foolish inability to act). The dream thus raises an issue that is evaded in Innocence: in what sense can distress be comforted by pity when the sufferer actually needs 'the lineaments of gratified desire'?[1] In 'A Cradle Song' the maker's smile 'beguiles' heaven and earth to peace, but here the dreamer's woe 'was neer beguil'd'. Instead, the comforted weeper develops an appetite for pity that displaces and represses desire. The image of the dreamer as a 'maiden Queen' also casts a new light on the vision of Innocence. The individual who believes that she is continually attended by a comforting protector becomes a monarch who can assume a right to such protection. The dream of comfort becomes a fantasy of power, in which the dreamer's maidenhood is implicitly the source and the instrument of her power. The Angel's role in relation to her is complex – servant, defender of chastity, sympathetic friend, object of desire, frustrated suitor and, finally, an enemy. The progress of the relationship illuminates not only the relationship between frustration and aggression, but also the psychological basis of spiritual values (as fear and secrecy transform the 'hearts delight' into a temptation that must be resisted, the good angel becomes an evil angel). The rapid departure of youth paradoxically confirms both the triumph and self-defeat of the maiden Queen. The speaker's inability to interpret her dream presages more 'Witless woe'.

The design above the text glows darkly. The golden-haired maiden Queen reclines in sorrow on a bed of shady green vegetation, turning away from her naked comforting Angel. Her languishing expression and the spikes of her golden crown are picked out clearly in ink. Above her a serpentine vine coils and twists. In this context her crimson and purple dress, like the pink in the Angel's dark flesh tones, suggests the burning of unsatisfied desire. Her open left hand at the Angel's sad face might be pushing him away, or making sure of his comforting presence, or doing both at once. He grasps her arm as if to coax and reassure. The composition creates a strong impression of enclosure: the dark tree at the left forms a smooth arch over the figures; sparse green foliage hangs down at top and right; behind the Angel a vague hedge or thicket rises darkly. The sky above burns orange, red and gold. There is gold in the Angel's hair, on his blue and brown wings, and in two dull streaks on the tree trunk.

The vine below the text that coils and forks by the last stanza recalls the serpent of desire on plate 31. A faint streamer from 'grey' has an arrow head, as if to emphasize the association between arming and ageing. Another arrow head appears in the left margin, beside 'Guarded' and 'Witless woe', while a sprig of ivy armed with small spikey leaves appears to the right of the title.

Less threatening, a vine springs into the right margin from 'day' in stanza 2, sprouting a single leaf among its coils and meanderings. The first three stanzas have a light covering of gold (at the right side), there is gold in the title and in the streamers at the bottom and left-hand side of the text. The upper part of the border is a green vine, which forms nine loops across the top of the plate, and three more either side. Below these at each side five green reeds grow out from the plate.

[1] See Blake's lyric 'What is it men in women do require' (*E* 474; *K* 184).

Plate 42: The Tyger.

Tyger Tyger. burning bright,
In the forests of the night;
What immortal hand or eye.
Could frame thy fearful symmetry?

In what distant deeps or skies.
Burnt the fire of thine eyes?
On what wings dare he aspire?
What the hand, dare sieze the fire?

And what shoulder, & what art,
Could twist the sinews of thy heart?
And when thy heart began to beat.
What dread hand? & what dread feet?

What the hammer? what the chain,
In what furnace was thy brain?
What the anvil? what dread grasp.
Dare its deadly terrors clasp?

When the stars threw down their spears
And water'd heaven with their tears:
Did he smile his work to see?
Did he who made the Lamb make thee?

Tyger Tyger burning bright,
In the forests of the night:
What immortal hand or eye,
Dare frame thy fearful symmetry?

When the child-like speaker of 'The Lamb' (plate 8) asks the creature 'Who made thee' there is no doubt about the answer. The Lamb seems a manifestation of the loving care of its maker, and the child feels a sense of identity with both creature and creator. But the speaker who confronts the Tyger struggles to come to terms with a creature that seems mysterious and terrifying. The question 'Did he who made the Lamb make thee' receives no answer. The poem brings into focus the shifting relationships between seeing and feeling in the *Songs*. In other poems the 'dreadful' aspect of the beast of prey undergoes a visionary transformation: in 'Night' the speaker's vision expands easily to accommodate the lion, which becomes a shepherd in 'New worlds'. The lion in 'The Little Girl Found' becomes a protective 'spirit arm'd in gold'. But in this poem the 'deadly terrors' of the Tyger resist the speaker's attempt to harmonize them with a benevolent conception of the world. From this point of view, the transformations in the other poems may appear evasive fantasies, which minimise the existence of real dangers. The converse also applies: from the point of view represented in 'Night', the speaker's vision in 'The Tyger' has contracted. Part of experience has become alien; the Tyger appears to live in an outer darkness, 'In the forests of the night'.[1] The question 'In what distant deeps or skies' presupposes a distant origin, whether celestial or infernal.

Such comparisons do not lead to a 'correct' view of the Tyger. They point instead to the relativity of vision, and to the mental strategies that determine patterns of belief. Here, the animal has become an enigma that the mind must struggle to contain, and the act of creation is accordingly imaged as a daring act of containment.[2] The violence of this act suggests not love, but an astonishing triumph of will – a will that seems embodied in the Tyger itself, whose heart-beats echo the beat of the creator's hammer, and whose eyes and body burn like the fires of the furnace. The creator of such a creature would seem to bear little resemblance to the intimate and protective maker of the Lamb. But the raging fire of the Tyger is also hard to reconcile with the more

[187]

abstract idea of creation as an orderly system which gives protection against chaos. This view of creation is evoked in the 'Introduction' of Experience, and in 'Earth's Answer', where it is associated with the stars and with 'selfish fear'. The Tyger seems to overwhelm all notions of creation as a defending order:

> When the stars threw down their spears
> And water'd heaven with their tears:
> Did he smile his work to see?

Chaos seems to be inside creation, not outside, appearing paradoxically within the 'fearful symmetry' of a 'deadly' creature. Seen in relation to Experience poems like 'Earth's Answer' or 'The Chimney Sweeper', this speaker's view of the Tyger is potentially liberating, as it threatens to undermine the mental foundations on which 'Starry Jealousy' has built its kingdom.[3]

The design gives very little sense of the speaker's breathless struggle. The pale shades of the sky and tree create an impression of lightness, even airiness, at odds with 'the forests of the night'. The Tyger itself, thick set and static, hardly seems threatening. Its wide eye and closed mouth give its a dolefully humorous look. The image dispels the impression of terror created in the song, and recalls the transformations in other poems (see plates 35 and 36). But something of the creature's demonic potential is suggested by the colouring: its body is lit from below, with black shadow falling on its back (an effect emphasized by the blue of the sky beneath its chest). It has no clear stripes, but mottles of yellow and gold, shading to crimson and dark blue. The leaves in the bottom left corner shine with gold before the animal's face (the one that grows up the left margin to join the first 'T' of the title is gold). Behind the Tyger the tree glows pink, and shadows fall on the wrinkled bark. Above the text, at the left a solitary bird flies up.

The title and the streamers that come from it are gold, and there are traces of gold on the fine branches between the stanzas. The border is unusually elaborate. From a stylized gold and green base with two arches, green branches develop, curving around the bottom corners and forming a loop either side of the tyger. Opposite the text trellises support plants whose leaves vaguely suggest flames. Around the top the trellis forms an inverted arch from which golden vines curl towards each other without meeting. The border recalls that on the combined title-page, and may associate the burning terrors of the poem with the exuplsion – or retreat – from Eden.

---

[1] In Blake's poem *Europe*, the 'forests of night' are associated with a contraction of vision, a fearful retreat from the 'infinite':

> Thought chang'd the infinite to a serpent: that which pitieth:
> To a devouring flame; and man fled from its face and hid
> In forests of night
>
> (*E* 63)

[2] Morton D. Paley in a detailed study of sources and influences, relates the presentation of the tyger here to contemporary ideas of the sublime, and argues that the beast is 'an incarnation of divine Wrath': *Energy and Imagination* (Oxford, 1970), pp. 30–60 (p. 59). For a selection of other views on this, the most discussed of Blake's poems, see *William Blake; 'The Tyger'*, edited by Winston Weathers (Columbus: Merrill, 1969).

[3] Ronald Paulson notes that the use of the tiger as an image of revolutionary violence 'was very much in the air' in the 1790s, 'Blake's Revolutionary Tiger', *William Blake's Songs of Innocence and of Experience*, edited by Harold Bloom (New York, 1987), p. 124.

A flower was offerd to me;
Such a flower as May never bore.
But I said I've a Pretty Rose-tree.
And I passed the sweet flower o'er.

Then I went to my Pretty Rose-tree:
To tend her by day and by night.
But my Rose turnd away with jealousy:
And her thorns were my only delight.

As a device used to define a human relationship, the image of the gardener tending a flower excludes the possibility of equality or independence. When the speaker of this poem rejects the offered gift, his sense of pride in his 'Pretty' Rose-tree implies possession. His protective management of the tree 'by day and by night' suggests a ritualistic devotion which transforms the loved one into an idol, and fosters the very jealousy it seeks to allay.

The scene below the text depicts an emotional stalemate. The languishing pose of the female at the right, the Rose-tree, echoes that of the maiden Queen in plate 41 (both women have red dresses). She looks sorrowfully away from her lover, who sits hunched over before a spiky tuft of grass, cradling his head in his arms, as if in despair. The sky above him glows with gold. Between them a large bird (perhaps a bird of paradise) and nine smaller ones fly up, emblems of the joy that both lovers turn away from. Three more fly upwards beneath the title (the largest is golden). The barren tree behind the woman offers no shade, although the vine which springs up from behind the tree and puts out a few small leaves is perhaps a sign of hope.[1]

The first letters of lines 1–3 are retouched in gold. In the last line the word 'my' is distinguished by a bold banner, emphasizing its importance in the poem. The title and the tendrils that sprout from it are gold, while the tightly coiled tendril which rises up the left margin from 'And' has some gold highlights at the top.

Ah! Sun-Flower

Ah Sun-flower! weary of time.
Who countest the steps of the Sun:
Seeking after that sweet golden clime
Where the travellers journey is done.

Where the Youth pined away with desire,
And the pale Virgin shrouded in snow:
Arise from their graves and aspire.
Where my Sun-flower wishes to go.

The speaker begins with a sigh which suggests the same weariness that he attributes to the Sun-flower (a suggestion emphasized by the heavy stresses in the song). The wistful tone and the implied sympathy for the time-bound victims are disarming. But as many critics have noted, the poem is not without irony.[2] Although the 'sweet golden clime' is introduced as a place of rest beyond time, the sense of timeless rest is soon complicated by the ambiguous syntax.[3] As lines 4 and 5 both begin with 'Where', the Youth seems at first to pine away 'Where the travellers journey is done'. This impression is reinforced by the verb 'aspire', which implies the continuation of unsatisfied longing. The speaker's relationship to the flower seems to parallel that between the loyal lover and the Rose-tree in the previous poem: there is an assumption of ownership ('my Sun-flower') which gives additional significance to his view that the flower 'wishes to go'. Like the youth and maiden, the speaker may be a victim of frustration; the 'sweet golden clime' can be seen as a symptom of repressed desire rather than an alternative to it.

The text and title appear in a cloud (which, as in plates 30 and 40, may indicate the speaker's confusion). In some copies a sun breaks through the clouds in the right margin, but this has been painted out here (*IB* 43). In the left margin, at the top of a tightly coiled tendril sits the tiny golden human form of the Sun-flower, with petal-like arm, root-like leg, and hair flowing back. There is gold in the title and the streamer above it, and in the coils of the serpentine vine at bottom right; gold shading appears to the left of stanza 1 and on the edges of the clouds at right.

The Lilly

The modest Rose puts forth a thorn:
The humble Sheep. a threatning horn:
While the Lilly white, shall in Love delight,
Nor a thorn nor a threat stain her beauty bright

Like 'The Angel' this song points to the close relationship between passive virtue and aggression. Modesty and humility depend on self-possession, which makes an enemy of impulse – in the self and in others. There is an implicit parallel between the attitudes represented by the rose and sheep, and the attitudes of the speakers in the first two poems on this plate: self-possession must lead to possessive relationships with others, confining desire and thus generating unsatisfied longings. In contrast, the Lilly represents a love that is neither self-denying nor self-protective.[4] The change in the metrical pattern after line 2 enacts a release, and throws emphasis on 'Love' (which appears for the first time on this plate). Unlike the speakers of the previous two songs, the speaker here does not use a possessive pronoun.[5]

There is room only for marginal decoration here. The Lilly hangs down over the text at the right, its leaves and blossom highlighted in gold. The Lilly's drooping appearance may seem to contradict the song's 'promise of immunity to threat' as Erdman notes, and certainly contrasts with the aspiring Sun-flower (*IB* 43). It is placed, though, among 'delight', 'beauty' and 'bright'. The text is framed at the bottom and left by a sturdy vine which sprouts near 'beauty' and hangs a golden leaf over 'modest'. There is gold in the title, in parts of the coiling tendril at its left, and on the vine in the left margin (which has a dark, bronze-like sheen). The green in the left margin and beneath the text, helps to balance the colour distribution of the plate as a whole.

The border is composed of an elaborate brown trellis. Green leaves and tendrils appear in the six recesses at either side; at the top, vegetation curves and billows around an inverted, flattened arch; at the bottom, vines from left and right each sport three tiny leaves inside another arch.

[1] In other copies the vine circles in front of the base of tree (see *IB* 43).

[2] See, for example, Harold Bloom, *Blake's Apocalypse: A Study in Poetic Argument* (London, 1963), pp. 139–40; D. G. Gillham, *Blake's Contrary States* (Cambridge, 1966), pp. 209–11; and the more detailed study by William J. Keith, 'The Complexities of Blake's "Sunflower": An Archetypal Speculation', in *Blake: A Collection of Essays*, edited by Northrop Frye.

[3] Gillham notes: 'There is no main verb in the long sentence which constitutes the song, because nothing is ever to come to a resolution', op. cit., p. 210.

[4] As Grant notes, the Lilly's delight contrasts with the self-denying attitude of the Clod of Clay (on plate 32). John E. Grant, 'Two Flowers in the Garden of Experience', *William Blake: Essays for Samuel Foster Damon*.

[5] Some critics find irony here, too: see John Holloway, *Blake: The Lyric Poetry*, p. 24. It is possible to see a circular pattern on the plate as a whole, the Lilly taking us back to the 'sweet flower' that is freely offered in the first poem.

Plate 44: The Garden of Love

I went to the Garden of Love.
And saw what I never had seen:
A Chapel was built in the midst,
Where I used to play on the green.

And the gates of this Chapel were shut,
And Thou shalt not, writ over the door;
So I turn'd to the Garden of Love,
That so many sweet flowers bore,

And I saw it was filled with graves,
And tomb-stones where flowers should be:
And Priests in black gowns, were walking their rounds,
And binding with briars, my joys & desires.

The enclosed space of the garden is a characteristic setting of Experience, in contrast to the open fields of Innocence. The speaker who goes to the Garden of Love apparently assumes that love is set apart from the rest of life. His compressed narrative develops another version of the garden/ desert antithesis explored in plates 34–36. While he emphasizes the difference between the garden and the graveyard, there is an implicit parallel between them. The closed chapel with its prohibitions is a manifestation of the same urge to set love apart in a special place and enclose it.[1] The vision of the garden as a graveyard where death is cultivated and where Priests are committed to a joyless ritual is a grim revelation of the consequences that flow from his own assumptions ('I . . . saw what I never had seen'). His fate parallels that of the speaker in 'My Pretty Rose Tree', who is rewarded with thorns.

The illustration above the text recalls the scene of mourning on the Experience title-page (plate 29). A boy and girl with ashen hair kneel in prayer with a bald priest. The children stare blankly into the dark mouth of a newly-dug grave, towards which the sorrowful priest gestures as he reads from his book. The grey tombstone leaning above the grave has a curved top, perhaps a heavy attempt at a floral pattern. Behind the figures thin black branches rise indistinctly into dark vegetation which admits no light. The dark window in the church seems opaque; the church wall is either cracked or lined with leafless creepers. In Innocence, death is seen as a liberation, an entry into new worlds. Here the emphasis is on confinement, as sorrow and fear dominate.

The text area combines opposite impressions. The serpentine earthworm that coils at the right of stanzas 1 and 2, and the smaller worms that divide the stanzas, evoke the horrors of the grave. But the pale blue and white colouring of the background suggests open sky. Beneath the text an indistinct grave mound appears with vague, curving briars; to its right flowers are just visible. There is gold in the title, above the grave mound, and along the right-hand edge of the plate (opposite lines 3–9). Around the text area, the border is a green trellis (reinforced at each side by a gold line); the upper border is composed of asymmetrical, serpentine leaf forms of green and gold. (There is some pencil smudging in the border left of the title, and brown paint or ink smudging right of the funeral mound.)

---

[1] Gardner suggests that the poem may allude to a contemporary event: 'A year before Blake issued *Songs of Experience* a chapel was built "on the green" in South Lambeth.' The South Lambeth chapel was erected for 'a very exclusive communion', as all members of the congregation had to be able 'to pay a rent for their places'. *Blake's 'Innocence' and 'Experience' Retraced*, p. 139.

[2] The motif of the grave bound with briars recurs in Blake's work as a symbol of repression. (See for example, the illustrations for *Night Thoughts*, 34, 35, 96.)

Plate 45: The Little Vagabond

Dear Mother, dear Mother, the Church is cold,
But the Ale-house is healthy & pleasant & warm:
Besides I can tell where I am use'd well,
Such usage in heaven will never do well.

But if at the Church they would give us some Ale.
And a pleasant fire, our souls to regale:
We'd sing and we'd pray all the live-long day:
Nor ever once wish from the Church to stray.

Then the Parson might preach & drink & sing.
And we'd be as happy as birds in the spring:
And modest dame Lurch, who is always at Church
Would not have bandy children nor fasting nor birch

And God like a father rejoicing to see.
His children as pleasant and happy as he:
Would have no more quarrel with the Devil or the Barrel
But kiss him & give him both drink and apparel.

In this song the speaker and his mother are presumably outcasts who have found more charity in alehouses than in churches.[1] The vagabond's assertion that ale and a pleasant fire 'regale' the soul cheerfully confounds the traditional distinction between body and soul.[2] His sense of good 'usage' strikes at the foundations of a theology that appears to sanctify repression and deprivation. From his point of view, the Devil is a vagabond – deprived of love, drink and apparel. A society that imagines such usage in heaven will 'never do well' on earth. The illustration above the text enacts his vision of forgiveness. The massive tree trunks at left and right recall the dark wood of 'The Little Boy found' (plate 14), while their canopy of leaves resembles those of the protective oaks on plates 6 and 8. The old man in the yellow robe who kneels protectively over a hunched, naked figure can be seen as 'God like a father' embracing a pathetic outcast, 'the Devil'. The old man's eye is golden, there is gold shading on his white hair and beard, and his halo sends fine golden rays across the tree trunks. The naked outcast also has a kind of halo – there is a bright glow of gold beneath his head (his hair, arm and back have gold highlights). If this scene represents the child's ideal, the scene below shows the grim reality in his world: a destitute family by a makeshift fire. At the right a mother (identified by her pink dress) crouches; her head is covered by a cowl which makes her seem withdrawn into despair. A naked child kneels before her, reaching up to her for comfort; another stands looking on by her left knee. To the left of the fire, the father kneels dejected, head propped on left hand; small stones or coals have been inked in by his trailing hand; the child at his side is an uncoloured, ghostly presence.

The gold in the title, and in the streamers above it, has been applied lightly. A vine curls down the right margin beside the first ten lines. Two small birds to the right of stanza 3 have been over-painted and are virtually indistinguishable. Two more, slightly clearer, offer a visual equivalent of the 'rejoicing' in stanza 4 (to the right of the first two lines). The willowy green fronds that droop from the top of the border may recall the protective curves of Innocence. The broken lines of the lower part of the border vaguely suggest leaves.

[1] Gardner suggests that 'Neither the boy, nor the mother he addresses, is a vagabond, since the church-going he cites was to the culpably destitute as alien and unthinkable as quilts and silk curtains': *Blake's 'Innocence' and 'Experience' Retraced*, p. 116. However, the child may be protesting about the indifference of the Church to the poor, rather than about 'churchgoing'.

[2] In *The Marriage of Heaven and Hell* the Devil claims that 'Man has no Body distinct from his Soul' (*E* 34; *K* 149).

Plate 46: London

I wander thro' each charter'd street.
Near where the charter'd Thames does flow
And mark in every face I meet
Marks of weakness, marks of woe.

In every cry of every Man.
In every Infants cry of fear.
In every voice; in every ban.
The mind-forg'd manacles I hear

How the Chimney-sweepers cry
Every blackning Church appalls.
And the hapless Soldiers sigh
Runs in blood down Palace walls

But most thro' midnight streets I hear
How the youthful Harlots curse
Blasts the new-born Infants tear
And blights with plagues the Marriage hearse

Only one of the poems of Innocence uses a particular location: 'Holy Thursday' refers to St. Paul's, into which Charity School children flow 'like Thames waters' (plate 19). Here the speaker shows an awareness of the commercial and legal basis of the city that is quite beyond the scope of Innocence. In his vision the Thames features not as an image of natural energy but as part of social system that seems profoundly unnatural. The recognition that all channels of communication are 'charter'd' might be reassuring to those who believe in the benefits of law and trade.[1] But to this speaker the city appears blighted by the institutions and beliefs that supposedly hold it together. There seems to be no possibility of escape from the 'mind-forg'd manacles', which exert their influence on every infant. The first two stanzas create an impression of universal imprisonment. The last two make specific connections between sources of oppression and victims: a church that condones brutal child labour, a monarchial state dependent on human sacrifice for its defence, marriage laws that promote prostititution and inheritable venereal disease. The insistent rhythms and arresting imagery give this indictment of contemporary London great emotional force but, as many critics have noted, the speaker seems ravaged by, or implicated in, the desolation he records.[2] Everything in his vision is reduced to 'one measure'.[3] If there is irony here, it doesn't necessarily weaken the force of his condemnation; it may confirm his view that the 'mind-forg'd mancles' can be heard in 'every voice'.

The illustration above the text modifies the impression created by the song. The scene is apparently a 'midnight street'. A shaft of light falls across a stone wall and closed door, onto golden cobbles (at right of the title). A young boy leads an old man on crutches. The man's flowing white hair and beard recall the God-like protector of the previous plate, but here marks of weakness and woe are all too obvious. The closed door may indicate the general lack of pity in this environment. But the orange-brown wall gives an impression of warmth, and the design provides an image of innocence and protective care that the poem itself makes no mention of.[4] If the adult speaker of the poem is detached in his judgements, the child here seems engaged – in an act of pity. Reversing the familiar pattern of the *Songs* the child is the guardian of the adult. The light green of the boy's costume contrasts with the dull blue of the man's, and adds a hint of natural freshness to the scene. To the right of stanzas 2 and 3 a naked boy – completely golden – kneels warming his hands at a glowing fire that forms a cloud of smoke above him. This image recalls the destitute family on the previous plate, but unlike that family, this vagabond doesn't

[193]

seem paralysed by misery. The gold here may suggest an innocence which, like the Chimney Sweeper's (plate 37), survives in the face of woe. (The turbulence of the smoke and flames may also recall the fires from which Adam and Eve flee on the combined title-page.)

The title is gold, and there is gold in the flames and smoke of the fire, in the left margin by stanza 3, and (a faint patch) below 'hearse'. At the foot of the page a serpentine line helps to define the text area. Below it green earth appears; some darker lines along the bottom edge of the plate (rising at the right) suggest slanting vegetation. The border is a simple brown rectangular frame. The short line and three circles on either side at the top may indicate drapery.

[1] The word 'charter'd' in the first stanza evokes the legal rights and privileges upon which the wealth of the city depends. More generally it points to the assumption that law is the guarantee of liberty. Glen notes that Thomas Paine had challenged the accepted meaning of 'charters' in *The Rights of Man*, Heather Glen, *Vision and Disenchantment*, p. 210.

[2] See for example, Raymond Williams, *The Country and the City* (London, 1975), pp. 142–52; E. P. Thompson, 'Blake's London', *Interpreting Blake*, ed. Michael Phillips (Cambridge, 1978), pp. 5–39; Edward Larrissy, *William Blake*, pp. 42–55.

[3] See *The Book of Urizen*, in which the fall begins with Urizen's attempt to reduce experience to 'One curse, one weight, one measure' (*E* 72; *K* 224).

[4] A similar image appears in *Jerusalem* plate 84. See *IB* 363.

Plate 47: The Human Abstract.

Pity would be no more,
If we did not make somebody Poor;
And Mercy no more could be.
If all were as happy as we;

And mutual fear brings peace;
Till the selfish loves increase.
Then Cruelty knits a snare,
And spreads his baits with care.

He sits down with holy fears.
And waters the ground with tears:
Then Humility takes its root
Underneath his foot.

Soon spreads the dismal shade
Of Mystery over his head;
And the Catterpiller and Fly.
Feed on the Mystery.

And it bears the fruit of Deceit.
Ruddy and sweet to eat:
And the Raven his nest has made
In its thickest shade.

The Gods of the earth and sea,
Sought thro' Nature to find this Tree
But their search was all in vain:
There grows one in the Human Brain

The song is a counterpart of 'The Divine Image' (plate 18).[1] In the Innocence poem the 'virtues of delight' are seen in relation to personal (and undefined) distress. Here the same virtues are seen in social terms, and in relation to human selfishness. The allegorical sequence presents a condensed social history that has some parallels with accounts by Enlightenment historians: it shares the common assumption that human communities originate in a condition of truce ('mutual fear'), and it relates psychological developments implicitly to changes in the method of sub-sistence.[2] Hunting with snares and baits involves not only cruelty, but also 'care' (carefulness, and uncertainty about the outcome). It requires patience, the ability to wait ('He sits down'), and in this condition of expectancy 'holy fears' appear: presumably fears of a divinity who must be appeased. In this way, the mental habits of the hunter prepare for those of the cultivator, whose activity depends on a settled way of life, involves more 'care' (he 'waters the ground with tears') and leads to the growth of passive virtues such as Humility. Thus moral and religious ideas are seen to arise in relation to particular activities, and religious 'Mystery' seems rooted in the historical progression towards civil society. The full-grown tree is an emblem of organized religion, supporting parasites (the Catterpiller and the Fly are perhaps emblems of priesthood), and fostering the fear of death (the Raven). The seductive fruit of Deceit, which corresponds to the forbidden fruit of Eden, is the final expression of the hunter's cruelty: it is the bait in a snare.

The historical process in this account seems governed by mental rather than material causes ('Cruelty' is responsible for most of the developments; the tree grows 'in the Human Brain'). Nevertheless, it is a deterministic vision of life, which leaves no room for the spontaneous joy of Innocence. In the first stanza pity is linked exclusively to poverty, a link which allows no recogni-tion of other kinds of distress, and gives no intrinsic value to pity and mercy. As in 'London' and other poems of Experience, the abstract and analytical approach to the human situation gives rise to penetrating insights, and to a sense of its own limitations.

The text appears between a grey, leafless tree at the right and another tree partly visible along the left side of the plate.[3] Rather like the composition of plate 36, this gives the impression of a deep, chasm-like space, at the foot of which, below the text, an old man kneels before a murky blue and brown mire. His white beard and blue robe recall the aged cripple of the previous plate. He grasps at ropes in a gesture that seems ambiguous – he could be struggling to free himself, or tying himself down, or both. One rope passes over his head, another appears to grow from it, as if 'mind-forg'd'. In the light of the poem he can be seen as a hunter caught in his own snare, Cruelty trapped beneath the shade of Mystery. The drooping bulrushes to his left may associate him with the Mosaic tradition.[4]

Gold appears in the title and in the banner that runs down from its first letter; there are gold highlights near the base of the tree to the right (suggesting the grain of its bark), more in the vegetation immediately below it, and some in the old man's beard. A line of gold runs down part of the edge of the plate at either side. The border has two elements: from the base, green and brown lines curve gently inwards at either side; spiky flame-like leaves appear at the top corners.

[1] 'A Divine Image' was also apparently composed as a counterpart to 'The Divine Image' in Innocence, but appears in only one copy (see Introduction).

[2] Blake could have seen comparable accounts of social development in, for example, Rousseau's *Discourse of the Origin of Inequality*, or Hume's *Natural History of Religion*. For a full discussion of contemporary views of the relationship between social structures and methods of subsistence, see R. L. Meek, *Social Science and the Ignoble Savage* (Cambridge, 1976).

[3] In some copies a raven is seen distinctly at the top of the tree on the right (see *IB* 47).

[4] See plate 13, where there is also, as here, a connection between mire and rushes.

Plate 48: Infant Sorrow

My mother groand! my father wept,
Into the dangerous world I leapt:
Helpless, naked, piping loud:
Like a fiend hid in a cloud.

Struggling in my fathers hands:
Striving against my swadling bands:
Bound and weary I thought best
To sulk upon my mothers breast.

'Infant Joy' in Innocence (plate 25) evokes the joy of a mother and a new-born child through a dialogue. In this counterpart poem only the child's point of view is represented. The change in perspective draws attention to the problems of interpretation that the first poem gently hinted at. The parents' loving care may seem tyrannical to the infant; an adult might interpret the child's sulking as affection. From its own point of view the child seems fundamentally misplaced in a dangerous world: 'like a fiend' that will be punished, and like the swaddled Jesus, born to be a victim.[1]

The illustration below the text excludes the possibility of material poverty (which might explain – or explain away – the apparent distress of the parents), and also prevents a simple interpretation of 'dangerous'. The well-furnished interior looks comfortable and secure. Visually the plate forms a counterpart to 'A Cradle Song' in Innocence (plate 17), and like that plate emphasizes woven materials: textiles, the wicker of the crib, the carpet. In the light of the poem, the protection that surrounds the child here must itself seem threatening, potentially stifling. The mother's red dress stands out glowingly against the blue of the background curtains, which close the child's vista. Her expression is enigmatic as she bends towards her baby.

Gold is used liberally to highlight the edges of the drapery and bedding here, and also shades the child's body and hair. In the title 'INFANT' is reinforced with gold, 'SORROW' is not. There is gold in the lines under the title, in the arrow form to its left, in the streamer to the left of stanza 1, along the top edge of the plate and along the left edge by the text panel. The simple orange drapery border has a slightly unfinished look: the symmetry breaks down in lower half, where there are some signs of pencil work.

[1] In the Old Testament clouds are frequently associated with theophany (e.g. Exodus 16.10). Here the image of the 'fiend . . . in a cloud' complicates the 'Innocent' view of the child as a manifestation of divinity. Gardner suggests that the reference to swaddling registers a protest against a lingering contemporary practice. *Blake's 'Innocence' and 'Experience' Retraced*, pp. 126–8.

Plate 49; A Poison Tree.

I was angry with my friend;
I told my wrath, my wrath did end.
I was angry with my foe:
I told it not. my wrath did grow.

And I waterd it in fears,
Night & morning with my tears:
And I sunned it with smiles,
And with soft deceitful wiles.

And it grew both day and night,
Till it bore an apple bright.
And my foe beheld it shine,
And he knew that it was mine.

And into my garden stole.
When the night had veild the pole;
In the morning glad I see,
My foe outstretchd beneath the tree.

The poison tree of this song recalls the tree of 'The Human Abstract' (plate 47). It is another baited snare, but while the speaker acknowledges the fears and 'deceitful wiles' that foster the tree, there is no acknowledgment of cruelty. He does not say whether he foresaw the outcome of the events he describes; his intentions are never clearly (or consciously) formulated. The lack of clarity here prevents us from seeing his narrative simply as a tale of revenge: he exercises self-restraint – it is his enemy who transgresses. A version of this song appears in Blake's notebook under the title 'Christian forebearance'. The correspondence between the poison tree and the forbidden tree in Eden implies that the Genesis myth promotes and expresses a deeply confused moral vision. As Gallagher says, the poem is 'a counter-myth which exposes the biblical narrative as a fraud by giving the "true" etiology' of the tree of knowledge.[1]

In its colouring this is one of the coldest plates in this copy of the *Songs*. Apart from the red-brown of the print colour, and the touches of gold, all of the hues are cool. A heavy branch from the leafless tree at the right hangs slanting twigs and rods over a death-grey naked body below. The outstretched arms of the corpse recall the body of the child at the foot of plate 33, and perhaps also the crucifixion. The approach of morning is indicated by gold at the horizon to the left and right. The text is almost enclosed by a thin branch that descends the left-hand margin to 'My' in last line, emphasizing the word's importance in the song.

There is gold in the title and in the fine branches that surround it, along the edge of the branch to the right of the text, and a few dull gold highlights on the branch to the right of the body. The border motifs form another poison tree: the brown and grey stems at either side have nodules like bamboo; they put out sharp thorns at top left and right.

[1] Philip J. Gallagher, 'The Word Made Flesh: Blake's "A Poison Tree" and the Book of Genesis' *Studies in Romanticism* 16 (1977), pp. 237–49 (pp. 237–8).

Plate 50: A Little Boy Lost

Nought loves another as itself
Nor venerates another so.
Nor is it possible to Thought
A greater than itself to know:

And Father. how can I love you,
Or any of my brothers more?
I love you like the little bird
That picks up crumbs around the door.

The Priest sat by and heard the child,
In trembling zeal he siez'd his hair:
He led him by his little coat:
And all admir'd the Priestly care.

And standing on the altar high.
Lo what a fiend is here! said he:
One who sets reason up for judge
Of our most holy Mystery.

The weeping child could not be heard,
The weeping parents wept in vain:
They strip'd him to his little shirt.
And bound him in an iron chain.

And burn'd him in a holy place.
Where many had been burn'd before:
The weeping parents wept in vain.
Are such things done on Albions shore.

In the 'Little Boy' poems of Innocence, as in 'The Little Girl Found', weeping leads to the re-union of child with parent through the agency of a protective saviour. There are no priests in these poems: they are concerned with faith that is discovered through personal experience. 'A Little Boy Lost' develops a contrasting pattern. Here faith has become institutionalized and transformed into an orthodoxy. The little boy is 'lost' as soon as he makes an appeal to personal experience. His claim that thought cannot know 'A greater than itself' implicitly denies the possibility of knowing and loving a transcendent God. The priest's reaction recalls Hume's reference to the vengeance that would fall on those who set up reason against 'mystery'.[1] In the face of 'Priestly care', weeping is quite ineffectual: 'The Weeping child could not be heard';

'The weeping parents wept in vain'. An orthodox conception of divine love is upheld without mercy. As in 'Infant Sorrow', the child is at once a fiend and like Christ (stripped and bound); his individuality has to be sacrificed. Blake's contemporaries would of course regard such practices as belonging to a barbaric past. But the final question points to the spiritual reality of contemporary England, where the theology of sin and retribution is still preached. Among Watts's *Divine Songs*, for example, children would find the following lines:

> What if his dreadful anger burn,
>   While I refuse his offer'd grace,
> And all his love to fury turn,
>   And strike me dead upon the place?
>
> 'Tis dangerous to provoke a God!
>   His power and vengeance none can tell!
> One stroke of his almighty rod
>   Shall send young sinners quick to hell
>
> Then 'twill for ever be in vain
>   To cry for pardon and for grace[2]

Visually the plate has an unnatural, dream-like quality. Below the text, figures robed in purple or blue kneel with heads bowed towards a fire. All have grey cowls which cover their heads completely; the two at the left press their hands against their hidden faces; so apparently does one at the right who rises as if in distress. Their postures suggest a blind cringing fear or humility before the fire of punishment. The yellow and red of the fire are thrown into relief by black flames and smoke. To the right of the text, spiky blue leaves dance like more flames. Their outlines and colour contrast sharply with the soft curves and pastoral hues of Innocence.

There is gold in the title; faint gold shading down the left-hand margin (top half), and to the right of the last two stanzas; traces of gold on the fire and on the cowls of the kneelers. A bracket from the word 'how' in line 5 seems to refer back to the previous line, as if asking how thought can know 'A greater than itself'. The border is a simple grey frame at top and sides. Within the frame black vines twist down either side. At bottom centre are two bulbs, from which shoots push out sideways towards vague leaves at the bottom corners, with two flowers or fruits springing up at either side. The bulbs, which resemble testes, indicate perhaps that the poem enacts a sacrifice of the spirit to the vegetable world (see, for example, *Milton*, 19:49–60; *Jerusalem* 67:35–68:9, and plate 52).

[1] 'Will you set up profane reason against sacred mystery? No punishment is great enough for your impiety. And the same fires, which were kindled for heretics, will serve also for the destruction of philosophers.' David Hume, *The Natural History of Religion*, in *The Philosophical Works*, edited by Thomas H. Green and T. H. Grose, 4 vols (New York, 1964), II, 342.

[2] From 'The Danger of Delay', Isaac Watts, *Divine Songs*, p. 229.

Plate 51: A Little Girl Lost

> *Children of the future Age.*
> *Reading this indignant page;*
> *Know that in a former time.*
> *Love! sweet Love! was thought a crime.*

In the Age of Gold,
Free from winters cold:
Youth and maiden bright.
To the holy light,
Naked in the sunny beams delight.

Once a youthful pair
Fill'd with softest care;
Met in garden bright.
Where the holy light,
Had just removd the curtains of the night.

There in rising day.
On the grass they play:
Parents were afar;
Strangers came not near:
And the maiden soon forgot her fear.

Tired with kisses sweet
They agree to meet,
When the silent sleep
Waves o'er heavens deep:
And the weary tired wanderers weep.

To her father white
Came the maiden bright:
But his loving look,
Like the holy book,
All her tender limbs with terror shook

Ona! pale and weak!
To thy father speak:
O the trembling fear!
O the dismal care!
That shakes the blossoms of my hoary hair

In 'A Little Boy Lost', the boy is destroyed by the 'trembling zeal' of the priest, whose cruelty is publicly displayed. Here the focus has changed to the internalization of restraint: lives are blighted by 'trembling fear'. Like 'The Little Girl Lost' (plate 34), this song begins with a prophetic voice which looks to a future Age that will be free of present constraints. Before the present situation is described, however, the song reaches back to an Age of Gold when there was no shame about sexual love. In stanza 3 the narrative properly begins. The reference to the 'holy light' here might lead us to think that the story is set in the golden age, but this impression is modified by the reference to the 'garden bright' and to the removal of 'the curtains of the night' (a hint of divesting). As stanza 4 makes clear, this couple have withdrawn into a private place, remote from parents and strangers, and the maiden is initially in a state of fear. They are already far from the innocence described in stanza 2. Although we are told that the maiden 'forgot her fear', the description of their relationship actually suggests that both boy and girl think their love is 'a crime'. They do not consummate it in 'the holy light', but agree to meet in darkness. There is little sense of spontaneous delight; instead the emphasis is on weariness. More like lost souls than joyful lovers, they meet where 'tired wanderers weep'. It seems that Ona is already a 'Little Girl Lost' when she meets her father. She is terrified not by his anger, but by his 'loving look'. The ambiguity here complicates the conclusion: her terror indicates her sense of guilt, propagated by 'the holy book'; but it also suggests that, in the light of her own furtive desires, no expression of love can now seem innocent. The father's reference to the shaken 'blossoms' of his hoary hair subtly underlines the sexual implication: the imagery suggests winter disturbed by feelings appropriate to spring.

In the design, the vine-encircled tree in the right margin stands out boldly against the pale shades of the sky. In some copies only the vine has leaves, and there is a clear contrast between the barrenness of the tree and the exuberant forms of life that surround it.[1] In this version it is sometimes hard to distinguish between the foliage of tree and vine as leaves and coiling tendrils push into the spaces left by the text. Leaves added in the top corners contribute to the general impression of natural abundance. A squirrel with a long bushy tail stretches in a fork of the tree near 'forgot her fear'. Higher up a tiny golden human figure stands (barely distinguishable) between the tree and vine near 'delight', recalling the protective, angelic forms of Innocence. Birds abound on this plate. Two appear dimly at the left of stanza 1. In the right margin, also faint, are: three by stanza 1 (the larger bird of paradise here is gold); three by stanza 4 (the larger two are golden); four by stanza 5; two by stanza 6 and eight below it (the four flying above the vine tendril are gold). Most are flying upwards. Although there are some bare branches, the exuberance of the design suggests the ever-present reality of the 'Age of Gold', from which the human figures of the poem are unnaturally excluded.

The title and tendril coming from 'G' (linking the 'GIRL' with 'Children of the future Age') are gold. The tree trunk is flecked with gold, there is gold shading on the squirrel, on the lower part of the vine and its first tendril, in the sky where the vine curves around the base of the tree, in the grass at the foot of the plate (in patches), and in a strip down the left-hand side of the plate. The orange border is formed by a straight line at top and bottom. At either side the simple pattern breaks by the second stanza, as if to emphasize the distinction between the Age of Gold, and the fallen age described in the rest of the poem.

[1] See *IB* 93. The vine circles the tree at the bottom, but does not cross the trunk higher up (as it does in other copies).

Plate 52: To Tirzah

Whate'er is Born of Mortal Birth,
Must be consumed with the Earth
To rise from Generation free:
Then what have I to do with thee?

The Sexes sprung from Shame & Pride
Blowd in the morn; in evening died
But Mercy changd Death into Sleep;
The Sexes rose to work & weep.

Thou Mother of my Mortal part.
With cruelty didst mould my Heart.
And with false self-decieving tears.
Didst bind my Nostrils Eyes & Ears

Didst close my Tongue in senseless clay
And me to Mortal Life betray:
The Death of Jesus set me free.
Then what have I to do with thee?

It is Raised
a Spiritual Body

This poem does not appear in early copies of the *Songs*. Its symbolism, and the style of the lettering of the plate, suggest a date later than 1803, although it may have been included earlier (see Introduction, n. 33). The cryptic use of biblical names is typical of Blake's later poems. Tirzah was the first capital of the northern kingdom of Israel. It was thus a counterpart to Jerusalem, the capital of the southern kingdom of Judah, with whom its beauty is compared in Song of Songs (6,4). In Blake's symbolism, Jerusalem becomes associated with spiritual liberty, Tirzah with material constraint. In Numbers 27:1–11, Tirzah is one of the five daughters of Zelophehad, who plead successfully for the right of female inheritance. Blake seems to have read this passage allegorically, as showing the triumph of the five senses over the human spirit. Tirzah becomes associated with the fallen realm of the senses: she is a power that seeks to imprison humanity in a vision of the body as finite and corrupt.

In addressing her, the speaker of this song claims to reject her vision. His words 'what have I to do with thee' echo the words of Jesus to his mother just before he turned the water into wine at

Cana (John 2.4). The speaker's view that the natural world must be 'consumed' corresponds to the traditional view of the Last Judgement, although here it could be interpreted in the light of Blake's conviction that creation is consumed as soon as individuals learn to look on it imaginatively.[1] The compressed version of human history that follows explains how Tirzah assumed her dominance. The account is illuminated by the words on the garment in the design below, which come from I Corinthians 15.44: 'It is sown a natural body; it is raised a spiritual body. There is a natural body, and there is a spiritual body'. These words are part of a passage in which Paul explains the resurrection and the relationship between the first Adam and the second, Jesus: 'The first man is of the earth, earthy; the second man is the Lord from heaven' (15.47). The speaker's vision of history reflects this conception of Jesus. Adam is the type of our mortal life – divided into male and female, falling into a knowledge of good and evil, fear of death, and the conviction that work is a punishment (Genesis 3.19). In this context, 'Mercy' allows the belief that humanity will eventually be redeemed or awakened from its sleep in the power of Tirzah. As the speaker believes that redemption has already been made available by the death of Jesus, the poem introduces an element that was absent from the Bard's vision in 'Introduction': a saviour who liberates by his own loving example rather than by his reproaches. The poem can therefore be seen as showing a clarification of vision, which brings the redeeming love typical of Innocence into Experience, and allows error to be consumed by a liberated imagination.

However, the speaker's words can also be seen in a quite different light. In Innocence reassurance comes from the vision of a maker who became a little child. The 'man of sorrows' is acknowledged, but it is the birth of Jesus, re-enacted in the present, rather than his death in the past, that brings joy. When the speaker in 'To Tirzah' says 'The Death of Jesus set me free', he adopts a contrary view of the saviour. In Blake's mythical history *The Four Zoas*, the crucifixion is heralded by the songs of Tirzah, and brings Jesus into the realm of repressive state religion (105:26 ff. *E*378; *K*349). The death of Jesus, it seems, may confirm the power of Tirzah, by reinforcing a self-denying attitude of life. The speaker's view of his redemption might be seen as the triumph, rather than the defeat, of Tirzah. We don't need to consult later works in order to see this. His question to Tirzah presupposes her presence; she dominates his vision of history, while Jesus is mentioned in passing, and in terms that imply his absence. The speaker's tone suggests both 'shame' (concerning his mortal life) and 'pride' (in his rejection of Tirzah). In spite of his assertions, he seems bound by the errors he defines. His situation seems comparable to those who worship 'God & his Priest & King' in the belief that they have been set free, and who remain in a cruel fallen world, anticipating a Last Judgement.

The illustration below the text would seem to support the latter view. A naked man, deathly grey, lies or sits back supported by two young women who wear contrasting colours and hair styles.[2] The woman at the left has a faint smile. The legs of the naked man are hidden, but appear to be reaching down into a grave. A brown spot on his chest (just below the woman's hand) could be a shadow or blood. The old man in yellow to the right, who resembles the aged figures on previous plates, stoops towards him with a pitcher. The quotation from I Corinthians appears lengthwise on the old man's robe (the 'y' of 'Body' is scarcely visible). A branch from the tree at the right extends over the heads of the entire group, displaying green leaves and seven dull golden fruits. The design can be seen as an image of the speaker's vision of the human condition. As the fruits indicate, the myth of Eden dominates here; fall and redemption are intimately related. Seen as an image of the fall, the design shows humanity 'sown in corruption' – in the act of being betrayed to the confinement of mortal life by Tirzah-like females and a God who baptises us into death.[3] In this case the image allows us to see what is implicit in the song: the 'Mercy' that changed death into sleep, and condemned us to joyless labour, is a cruel one that uses Tirzah as its instrument. Seen as an image of redemption, the design shows humanity 'Raised a Spiritual Body' – being brought back from the grave like Lazarus (whose two sisters

[201]

had faith in his resurrection). It also shows that the saviour who presides over this vision of liberty is not Jesus, but his Father, the God who promotes the vision of human nature as sinful.

The plate is rich and glowing, with a symmetry in the colouring: the yellow at top left and bottom right (in the robe) is in balance with the blue at top right and lower left. Gold appears in the title (which is not very distinct), in faint curving lines either side of the text, in the hair of the women and the old man, in the yellow of the sky (bottom left). There are faint traces of gold on the old man's robe and beneath the jug, fine gold lines on the ground beneath the woman at the left and the corpse, highlights on the woman's right hand and her sleeves. Inside the grey brown rectangle of the border, a serpentine green vine descends either side of the text, terminating in tiny leaves. Unerased pencil lines, sketching other vines at top left, and some brown speckles of paint outside the plates, give the border an unfinished appearance.

[1] See *The Marriage of Heaven and Hell*, plate 14 (*E* 39, *K* 154).

[2] Keynes sees the women as 'Mother-love and Sex-love' who failed to save man, *Blake: Songs of Innocence and of Experience*, plate 52.

[3] Lindsay suggests that the women can be seen as Rahab and Tirzah, *Blake: Songs of Innocence and Experience*, p. 83. In Blake's symbolism, Rahab is an emblem of repressive state religion.

Plate 53: The School Boy

I love to rise in a summer morn,
When the birds sing on every tree;
The distant huntsman winds his horn,
And the sky-lark sings with me.
O! what sweet company.

But to go to school in a summer morn,
O! it drives all joy away;
Under a cruel eye outworn.
The little ones spend the day,
In sighing and dismay.

Ah! then at times I drooping sit,
And spend many an anxious hour,
Nor in my book can I take delight,
Nor sit in learnings bower,
Worn thro' with the dreary shower.

How can the bird that is born for joy,
Sit in a cage and sing.
How can a child when fears annoy.
But droop his tender wing.
And forget his youthful spring.

O! father & mother. if buds are nip'd,
And blossoms blown away,
And if the tender plants are strip'd
Of their joy in the springing day,
By sorrow and cares dismay.

How shall the summer arise in joy.
Or the summer fruits appear.
Or how shall we gather what griefs destroy
Or bless the mellowing year.
When the blasts of winter appear.

This song was originally included in Innocence. Presumably it was transferred to Experience because it is a song of protest; unlike the speakers of Innocence, the School Boy is not reconciled to the contraints imposed on him by others. He does not complain about books or learning, but about joyless and cruel methods of instruction which blight the spirit of enquiry. He already sees in the cycle of nature a pattern that will govern his life: the 'blasts of winter' are inevitable. But school seems unnatural because it exposes children to wintry conditions in their 'youthful spring'.

The playful activities and the costumes in the design testify to its origins in Innocence. The intertwining trees in the right margin recall the more regular trees on plate 4 (the 'Introduction' to Innocence). A grapevine sends out leaves and tendrils around them. In this composition study and play are closely related. At the top, the trees become 'learnings bower': a boy in yellow sits comfortably in a fork, reading a book. Below him three other boys are playing: one in red climbs or swings with legs outstretched; one in yellow clambers up; one in blue reaches up as if to take a firm grip on both trees.[1] On the ground three boys play at marbles. In the left margin, in a fork of the slender, vine-encircled tree leans an angelic figure in a white and yellow robe (seen indistinctly opposite stanza 4); higher up, by stanza 1, a bird of paradise appears with wings outstretched (reinforced with ink, but still difficult to see). The darker shades in the left margin balance the costumes at right.

In the title, 'The', 'S' (of 'School') and 'Boy' are gold, and the banners under the title have some gold in them. The reading boy has highlights in his costume; there is gold in the spikes of grass at the foot of the tree, and on the ground beneath marble players. In the upper border, green willowy fronds overlap, and curl around the top corners; black curling roots or leaves appear at the bottom.

[1] In some copies this figure's left arm becomes part of the tree, and a bunch of grapes appears above him near the right edge of the plate (*IB* 53).

Plate 54: The Voice of the Ancient Bard.

> Youth of delight come hither.
> And see the opening morn,
> Image of truth new born.
> Doubt is fled & clouds of reason.
> Dark disputes & artful teazing,
> Folly is an endless maze,
> Tangled roots perplex her ways,
> How many have fallen there!
> They stumble all night over bones of the dead:
> And feel they know not what but care;
> And wish to lead others when they should be led

Like the previous poem this song was originally included in the Innocence series. In its present position it ensures that Experience ends as it began, with the voice of a bard who speaks of daybreak. In contrast to the anguished hope of the 'Introduction', the bard of this song speaks with conviction of a new age that has actually dawned. The poem can be seen as a triumphant conclusion to the work as a whole, a confirmation that the passage through Experience can lead to a cleansing of perception. But if the song begins joyfully, the bard's attention soon turns from the 'Image of truth new born' to the error that 'is fled'. Denunciation seems to come more easily to him than the celebration of joy, and the irregular rhythms of his song appear to enact the stumbling he describes. The last line may reflect ironically on his own situation, and make us think of the design of plate 46 ('London'), in which a young child leads a elderly cripple with flowing white hair and beard.

The accompanying design also seems ambiguious. Below the text, the white bearded Bard stands playing on a harp amid a group of youths. The yellow of his robe and harp associate him with the approaching dawn at the right. The array of costumes makes this a particularly colourful scene. The young woman in yellow at the right has a faint smile. The figure in blue at the left, who embraces the girl in pink, also smiles, although the girl seems to be looking away. The kneeling figure in violet raises a hand, perhaps in wonder. Apart from these details, there is little visible delight here. The Bard dominates the group. The straight lines of the tall harp contrast with the curving foliage of the plate. The listening group is static.[1] One may recall the unused motto to the songs, which begins: 'The Good are attracted to men's perceptions / And think not for themselves'.

Gold has been used plentifully here: in the title, the flourish at left of 'Ancient', the leaves to the right of the text and in their circling stems; in the Bard's hair and beard in his robe and along the frame of his harp. The girl standing at far right has golden rays of dawn behind her head; more gold shines in the sky behind her. The border announces the end of the series with a unique flourish: a branch from the palm tree at the right curves into it, while the triple leaf form to the right of the text sprouts from it at top right (in other copies this form sprouts near 'hither'). The trellis has vines at the top and left, and there is a suggestion of roots at the bottom.

[1] Gleckner comments: 'If they are the youth of delight in the text, their delight is restrained indeed – to the point of indecipherable soberness'. Robert F. Gleckner, 'The Strange Odyssey of Blake's "The Voice of the Ancient Bard" ', *William Blake's 'Songs of Innocence and of Experience'*, edited by Harold Bloom (New York, 1987), p. 118.

Appendix

Extract from Laura Mary Forster's letter to E. M. Forster, dated 14 May 1923.

I hear that Alfred Storey in his life of Linnell, says that your copy of Blake's songs was sold not given to Bishop Jebb. I do not know his authority for contradicting Gilchrist who gives the true version, viz that Bishop Jebb on being asked to buy some [of] the drawings Mrs Blake had, in extreme poverty, decided to sell if she could, and that the Bishop said he was not a collector but would gladly *give* £21 towards the widow's support.

I am probably the oldest person who knows much verbally about this question [.] I often talked about Blake and the Songs of Innocence & Experience my Father left me, with Mr. Richmond. The last time I did this was when Mr. Richmond spent a week here in 1881. He took the book out of the shelf to look at it, as he used to do at Stisted Rectory, only there it lay invariably on the drawing room table. He had often spoken of Mrs Blake's having said she wished the Bishop to accept it not as a work of art, but as a token of gratitude, and hoped he would care for it as being her husband's own copy of his favourite work. Mr Richmond did not like all the decorations outside the pictures, and said Mrs Blake's gratitude was so great that he thought she had added them after Blake's death, and just before sending the work to Bishop Jebb, in order to enhance their beauty.

Works Cited

Adlard, John, *The Sports of Cruelty* (London, 1972).

Baine, Rodney M., with the assistance of Mary R. Baine, *The Scattered Portions* (Athens, Georgia, 1986).

Barbauld, Anna Laetitia, *Hymns in Prose for Children* (London, 1781).

Bass, Eben, '*Songs of Innocence and of Experience:* The Thrust of Design', in Erdman and Grant (1973): 196–213.

Behmen, Jacob, *The Works of Jacob Behmen, The Teutonic Philosopher*, ed. George Ward and Thomas Langcake, 4 vols (London, 1764–81).

Bentley, G. E. Jr., ed., *Blake Records* (Oxford, 1969).
——, ed., *Blake Books* (Oxford, 1977).

Bindman, David, *Blake as an Artist* (Oxford, 1977).
——, *The Complete Graphic Works of William Blake* (London, 1978).
——, *William Blake: His Art and Times* (New Haven and Ontario, 1983).

Bloom, Harold, *Blake's Apocalypse: A Study in Poetic Argument* (London, 1963).
——, ed., *William Blake's 'Songs of Innocence and of Experience'* (New York, 1987).

Blunt, Anthony, *The Art of William Blake* (Columbia, 1959).

Bunyan, John, *A Book for Boys and Girls* (London, 1686).

Butlin, Martin, *The Paintings and Drawings of William Blake*, 2 vols (New Haven and London, 1981).
——, 'The Physicality of William Blake: The Large Color Prints of "1795"', *Huntingdon Library Quarterly*, 52 (1989).

Chayes, Irene H., 'Little Girls Lost: Problems of a Romantic Archetype', in Frye (1966): 65–78.
——, 'The Presence of Cupid and Psyche', in Erdman and Grant (1970): 214–43.

Dossie, Robert, *The Handmaid to the Arts* (London, 1764).

England, Martha Winburn, and John Sparrow, *Hymns Unbidden: Donne, Herbert, Blake, Emily Dickinson and the Hymnographers* (New York, 1966).

Erdman, David V., *The Illuminated Blake* (London, 1975).
——, ed., *The Complete Poetry and Prose of William Blake* (New York, 1982).
——, and John E. Grant, eds., *Visionary Forms Dramatic* (Princeton, 1970).

Essick, Robert N., *William Blake, Printmaker* (Princeton, 1980).
——, *William Blake and the Language of Adam* (Oxford, 1989).

Frosch, Thomas R., 'The Borderline of Innocence and Experience', *Approaches to Teaching Blake's 'Songs of Innocence and of Experience'*, ed. Robert F. Gleckner and Mark L. Greenberg (New York, 1989): 74–9.

Frye, Northrop, 'Blake's Introduction to Experience', *Blake: A Collection of Critical Essays* (New Jersey: Englewood Cliffs, 1966).

Fuller, David, *Blake's Heroic Argument* (Beckenham, 1988).

Gallagher, Philip J., 'The Word Made Flesh: Blake's "A Poison Tree" and the Book of Genesis', *Studies in Romanticism* 16 (1977): 237–49.

Gardner, Stanley, *Infinity on the Anvil* (Oxford, 1954).
——, *Blake* (London, 1968).
——, *Blake's 'Innocence' and 'Experience' Retraced* (London and New York, 1986).

Gilchrist, Alexander, *Life of William Blake* (London, 1866).

Gillham, D. G., *Blake's Contrary States* (Cambridge, 1966).

Gleckner, Robert F., *The Piper and the Bard* (Detroit, 1959).
——, *Blake's Prelude* (Baltimore and London, 1982).
——, 'The Strange Odyssey of Blake's "The Voice of the Ancient Bard" ', in Bloom (1987).

Glen, Heather, *Vision and Disenchantment* (Cambridge, 1983).

Grant, John E., 'Interpreting Blake's "The Fly" ', in Frye (1966): 32–55.
——, 'Two Flowers in the Garden of Experience', in Rosenfeld (1966): 333–67.

Hagstrum, Jean, 'William Blake's "The Clod and the Pebble" ', *Restoration and Eighteenth-Century Literature: Essays in Honour of Alan Dugald McKillop*, ed. Carroll Camden (Chicago, 1963): 381–8.
——, 'The Fly', in Rosenfeld (1966): 368–82.

Hirsch, E. D., *Innocence and Experience* (New Haven and London, 1964).

Hirst, Désirée, *Hidden Riches: Traditional Symbolism from the Renaissance to Blake* (London, 1964).

Hume, David, *The Philosophical Works*, ed. Thomas H. Green and T. H. Grose, 4 vols (New York, 1964).

Jones, M. G., *The Charity School Movement* (Cambridge, 1938).

Keith, William J., 'The Complexities of Blake's "Sunflower": An Archetypal Speculation', in Frye (1966): 56–64.

Keynes, Geoffrey, *Blake: Songs of Innocence and of Experience* (London, 1970).
——, ' "Blake's Own" Copy of Songs of Innocence and of Experience', *The Book Collector* 29 (1980): 202–7.
——, ed., *Blake: Complete Writings* (Oxford, 1972).
——, ed., *The Letters of William Blake* (Oxford, 1980).

Langland, Elizabeth, 'Blake's Feminist Revision of Literary Tradition in "The Sick Rose" ', *Critical Paths: Blake and the Argument of Method*, ed. Dan Miller, March Bracher and Donald Ault (London, 1987): 225–43.

Larrissy, Edward, *William Blake* (Oxford, 1975).

Leader, Zachary, *Reading Blake's Songs* (London, 1981).

Leavis, F. R., *Revaluation* (London, 1936).

Lindsay, David W., *Blake: Songs of Innocence and Experience* (London, 1989).

Lowery, Margaret, *Windows of the Morning* (New Haven, 1940).

Meek, R. L., *Social Science and the Ignoble Savage* (Cambridge, 1976).

Mitchell, W. T. J., *Blake's Composite Art* (Princeton, 1978).

Nurmi, Martin K., 'Fact and Symbol in "The Chimney Sweeper" of Blake's *Songs of Innocence*', in Frye (1966): 15–22.
——, *William Blake* (Kent State, 1976).

Ostriker, Alicia, *Vision and Verse in William Blake* (Madison, 1966).

Paley, Morton D., *Energy and Imagination* (Oxford, 1970).
—— and Michael Phillips, eds., *Essays in Honour of Sir Geoffrey Keynes* (Oxford, 1973).
——, 'A New Heaven Is Begun: Blake and Swedenborgianism', in *Blake: An Illustrated Quarterly* 12, no 2 (1979): 64–90.

Paulson, Ronald, 'Blake's Revolutionary Tiger', in Bloom (1987).

Pinto, Vivian de Sola, 'William Blake, Isaac Watts, and Mrs Barbauld', in *The Divine Vision: Studies in the Poetry and Art of William Blake*, ed. Vivian De Sola Pinto (London, 1957).

Phillips, Michael, 'Blake's Early Poetry', in Paley and Phillips (1973).

——, 'William Blake and the "Unincreasable Club": The Printing of *Poetical Sketches*', *Bulletin of the New York Public Library* (1976).

——, 'William Blake's *Songs of Innocence and of Experience* from Manuscript Draft to Illuminated Book', *The Book Collector* 28 (1979): 17–59.

——, ed., *An Island in the Moon* (Cambridge, 1987).

Plumb, J. H., 'The New World of Children in Eighteenth-Century England', *Past and Present* 67 (May 1975).

Raine, Kathleen, *Blake and Tradition*, 2 vols (London, 1969).

Riffaterre, Michael, 'The Self-sufficient Text', *Essential Articles for the Study of William Blake, 1970–1984*, ed. Nelson Hilton (Connecticut: Hamden, 1986).

Rosenfeld, Alvin H., *William Blake: Essays for Samuel Foster Damon* (Providence, 1969).

Shrimpton, Nick, 'William Blake: Hell's Hymnbook', *Literature of the Romantic Period 1750–1850*, ed. R. T. Davies and B. G. Beatty (Liverpool, 1976): 19–35.

The Speaker: or Miscellaneous Pieces . . . to facilitate the improvement of Youth in reading and writing (London, c1780).

Thompson, E. P., *The Making of the English Working Class* (Harmondsworth, 1968).

——, 'Blake's London', *Interpreting Blake*, ed. Michael Phillips (Cambridge, 1978): 5–31.

Tolley, Michael J., 'Blake's Songs of Spring', in Paley and Phillips (1973): 96–128.

Viscomi, Joseph, *The Art of William Blake's Illuminated Books* (Manchester, 1983).

——, 'Recreating Blake's Illuminated Prints: The Facsimiles of the Manchester Etching Workshop', *Blake: An Illustrated Quarterly* 19 (1985).

Wagenknecht, David, *Blake's Night: William Blake and the Idea of Pastoral* (Cambridge Mass. 1973).

Watts, Isaac, *Divine Songs*, ed. J. H. P. Padford (Oxford, 1971).

Weathers, Winston, ed., *William Blake: 'The Tyger'* (Columbus: Merrill, 1969).

Wesley, John and Charles, eds., *A Collection of Psalms and Hymns* (London, 1741).

——, *A Collection of Psalms and Hymns*, tenth edition (London, 1779).

Wesley, John, ed., *A Collection of Hymns* (London, 1781).

Wicksteed, Joseph H., *Blake's Innocence and Experience* (London, 1928).

Williams, Raymond, *The Country and the City* (London, 1975).

Wynne, John, *Choice Emblems . . . for the Improvement and Pastime of Youth* (1772).